Kids Coloring Pad

Space, Sharks, Sports, and More

Coloring Pages for Kids

Coloring Pages for Kids
An imprint of Ciparum LLC

Kids Coloring Pad Space, Sharks, Sports, and More
© 2017 Ciparum LLC
All rights reserved.
ISBN-10:1-63589-494-8
ISBN-13:978-1-63589-494-3

Coloring Pages for Kids

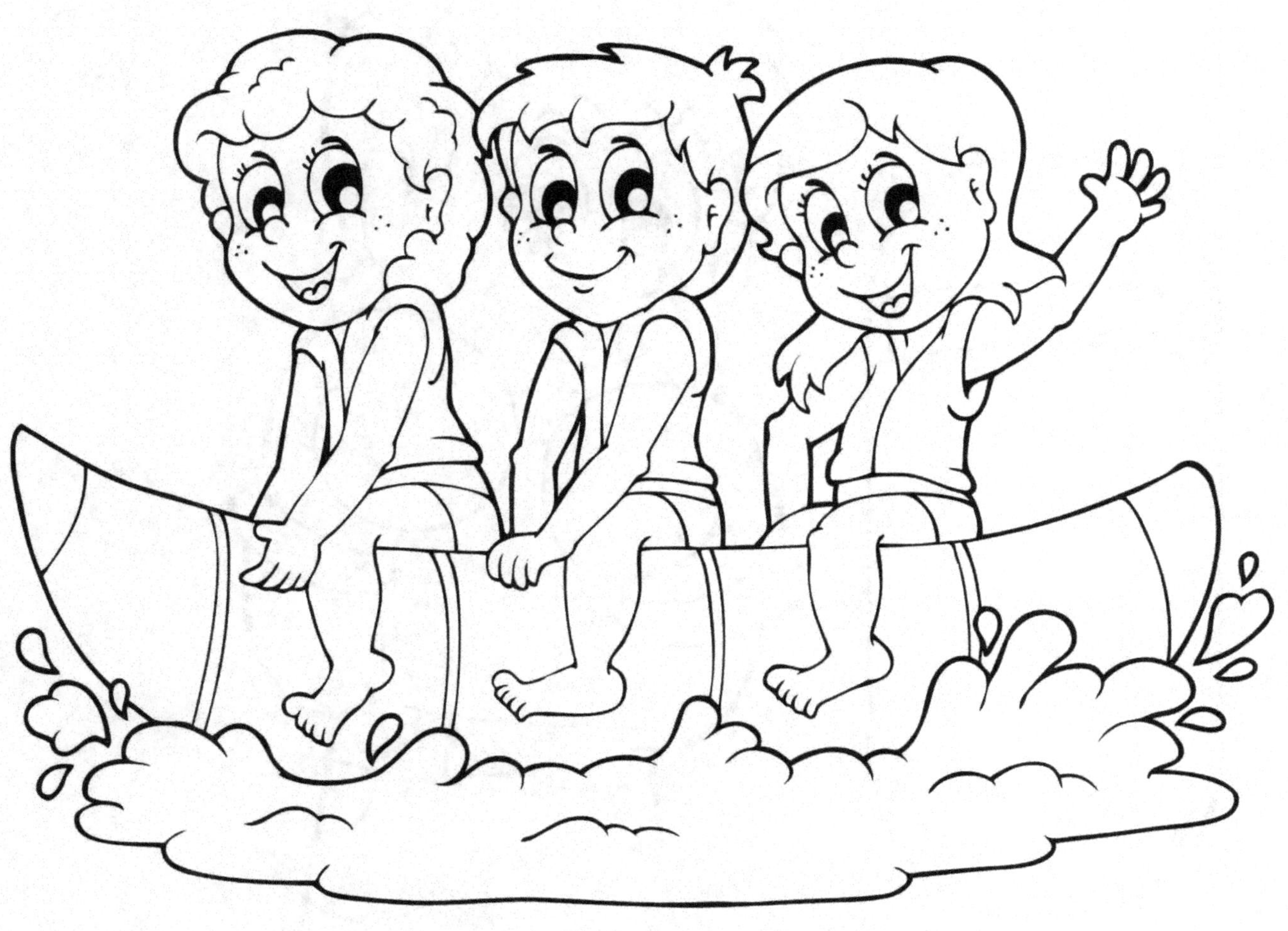

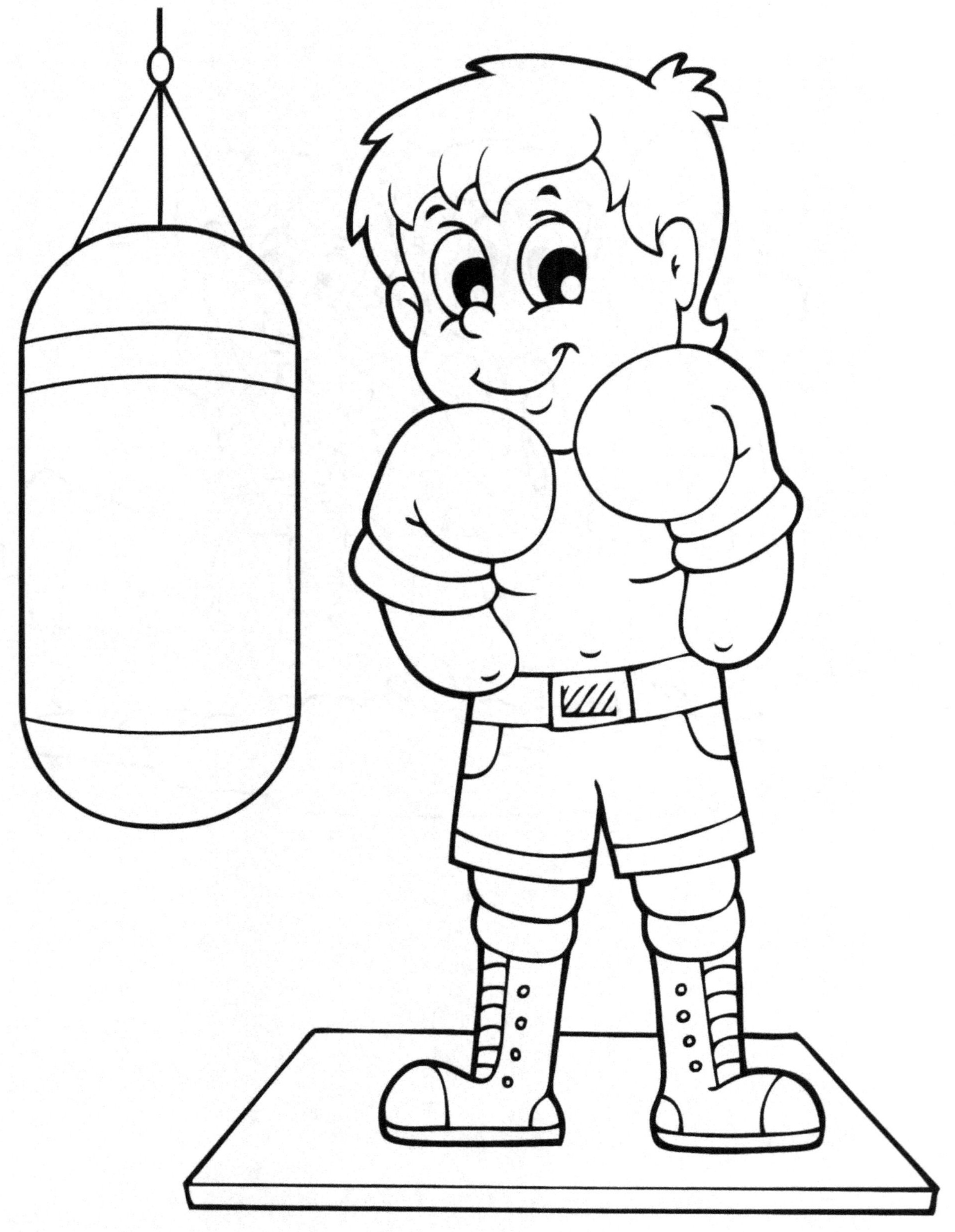

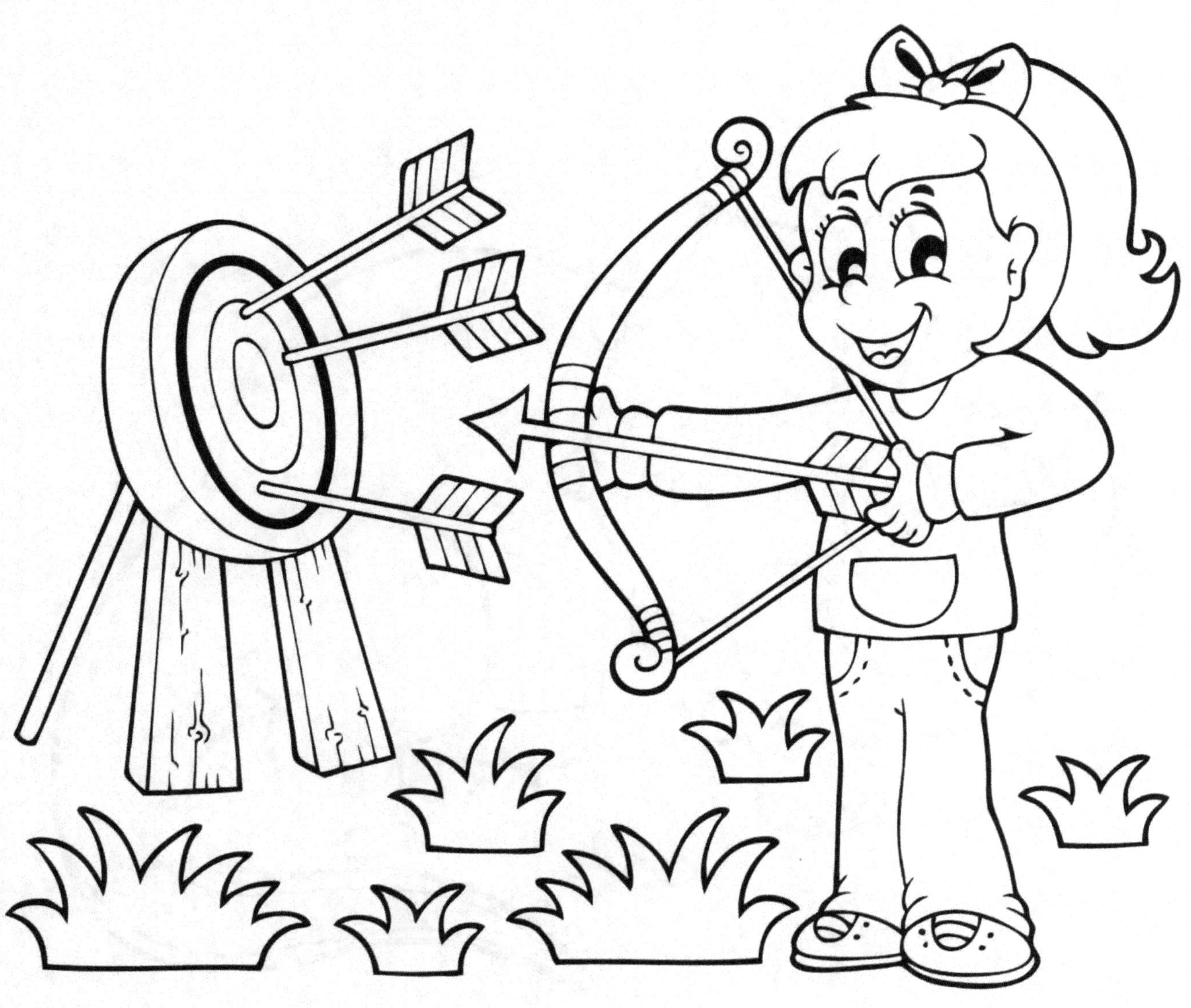

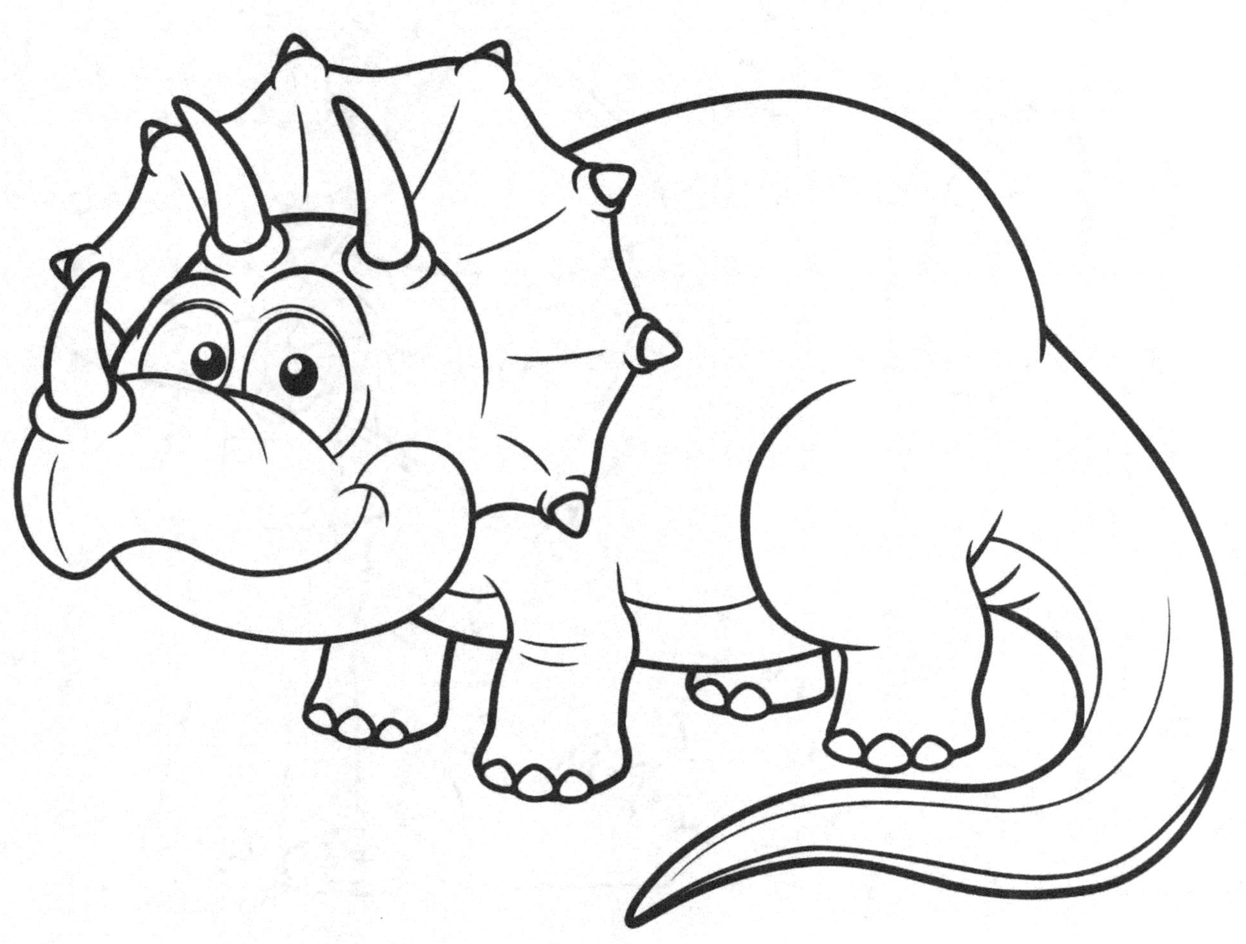

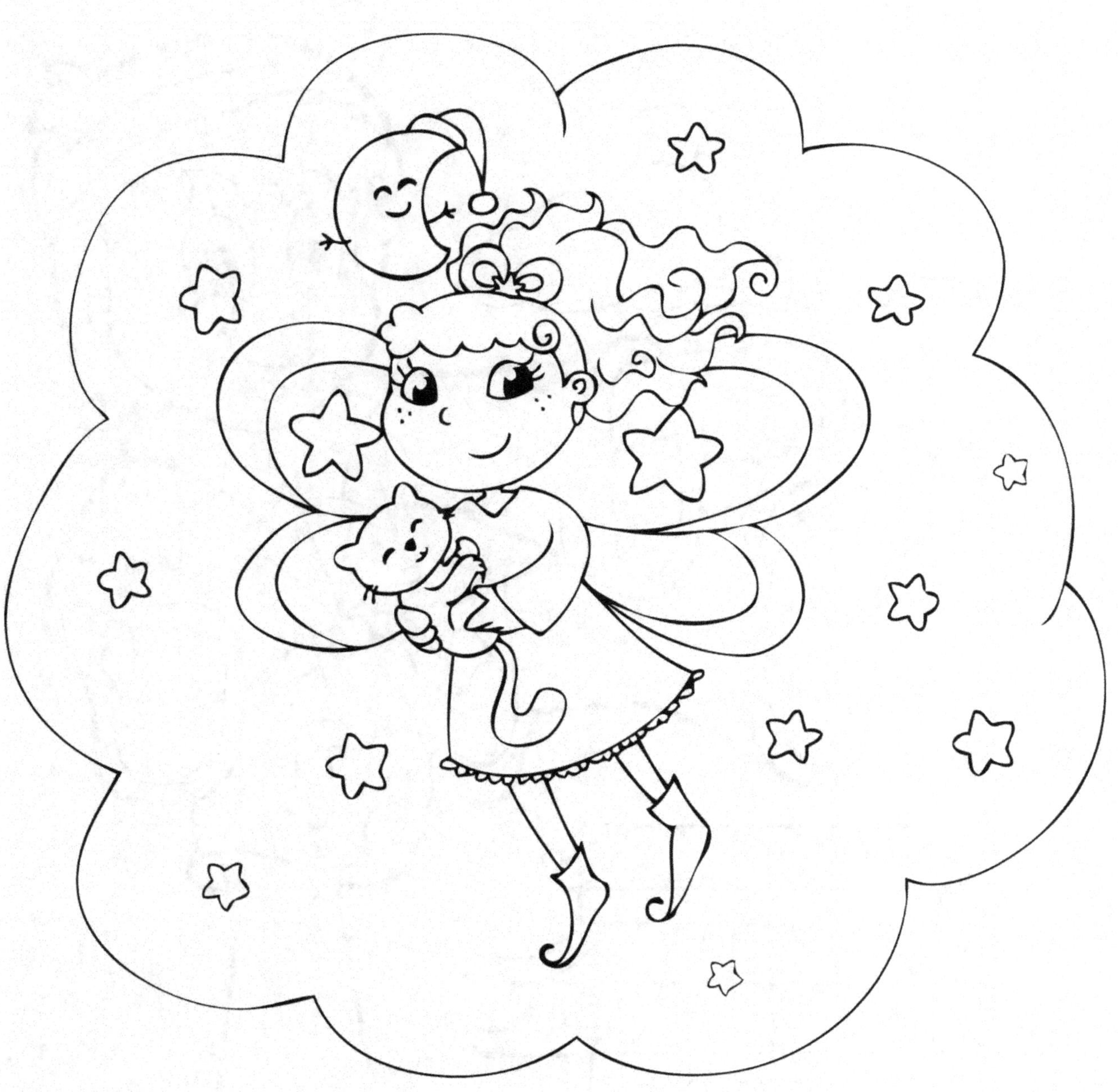

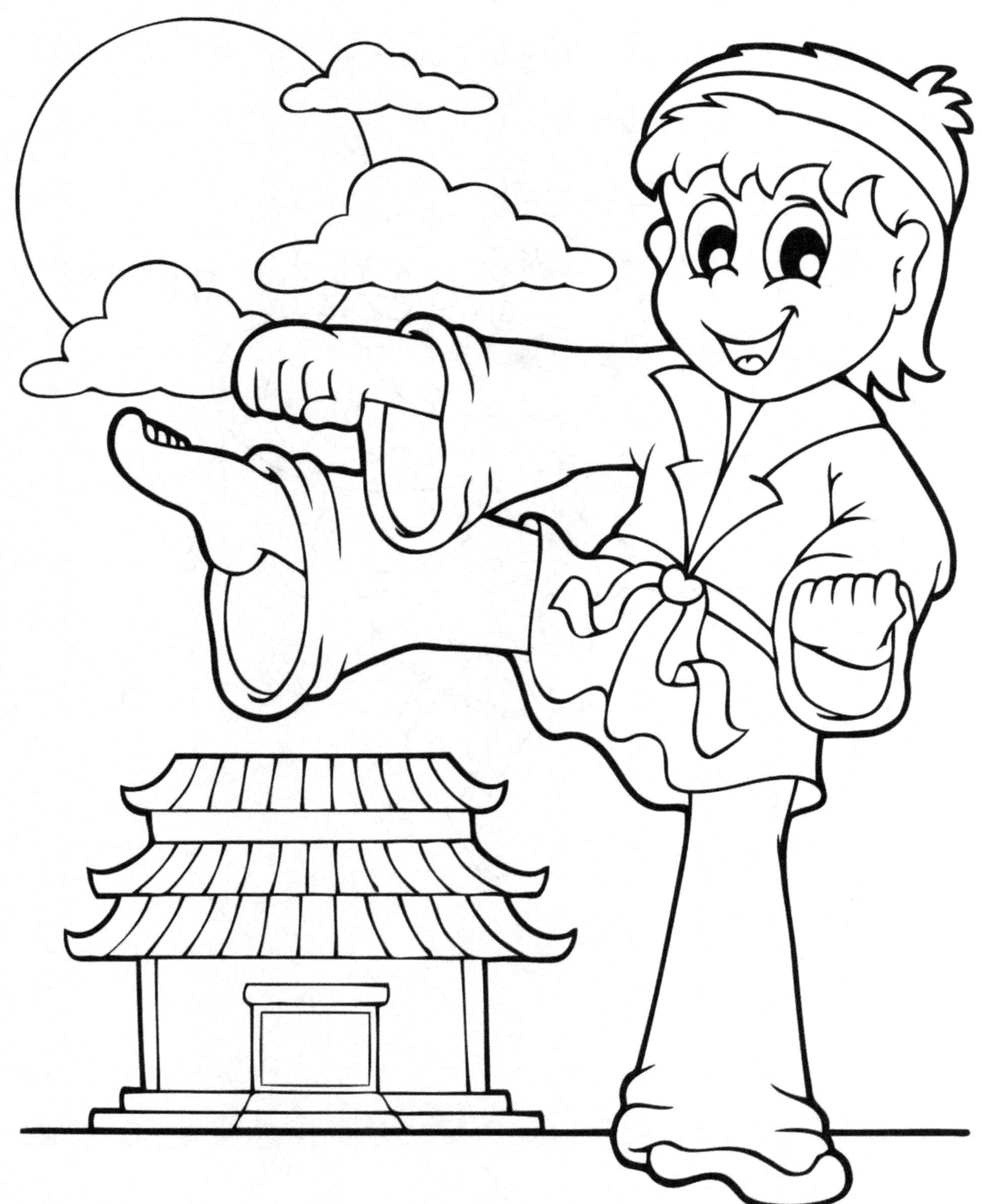

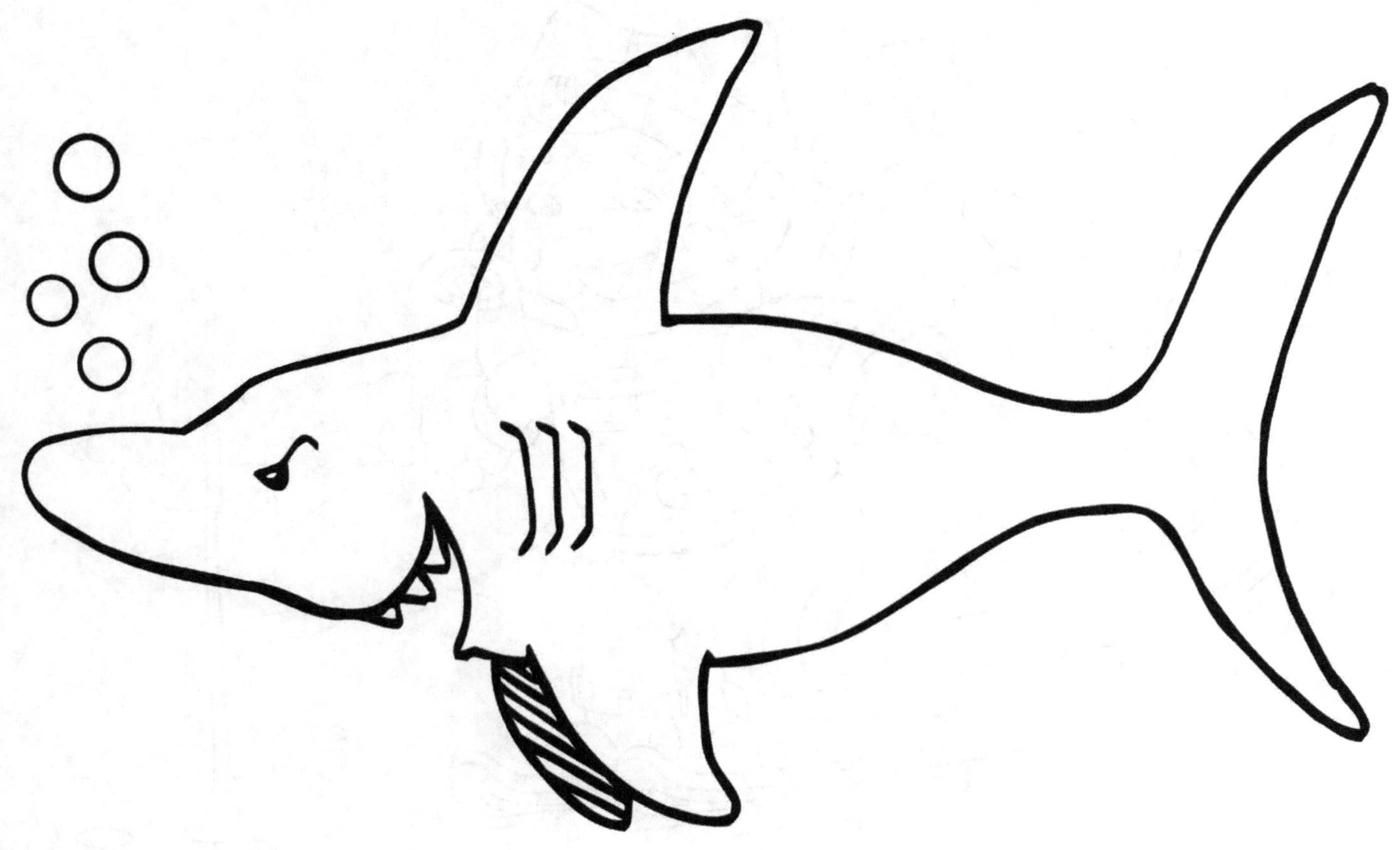

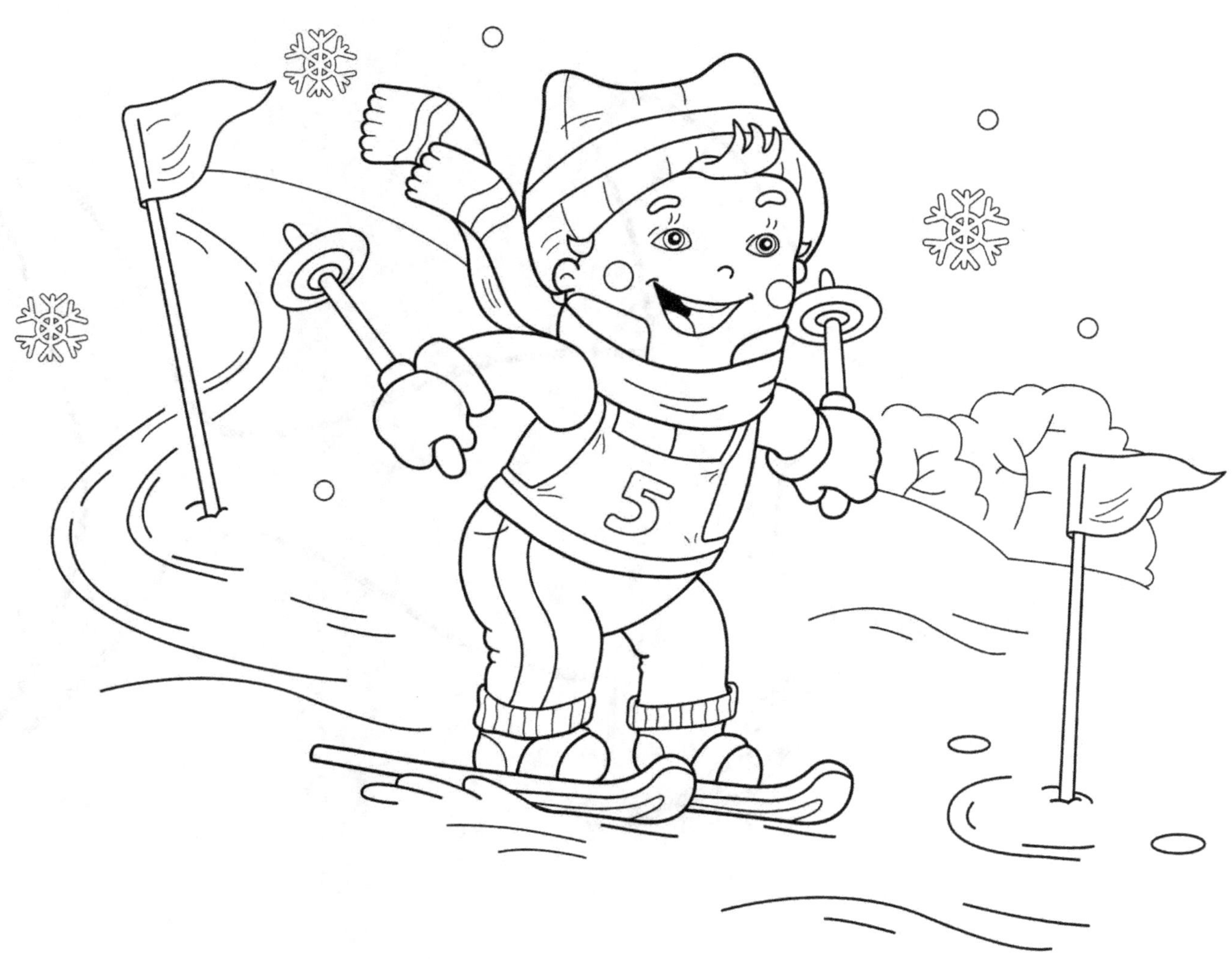

5

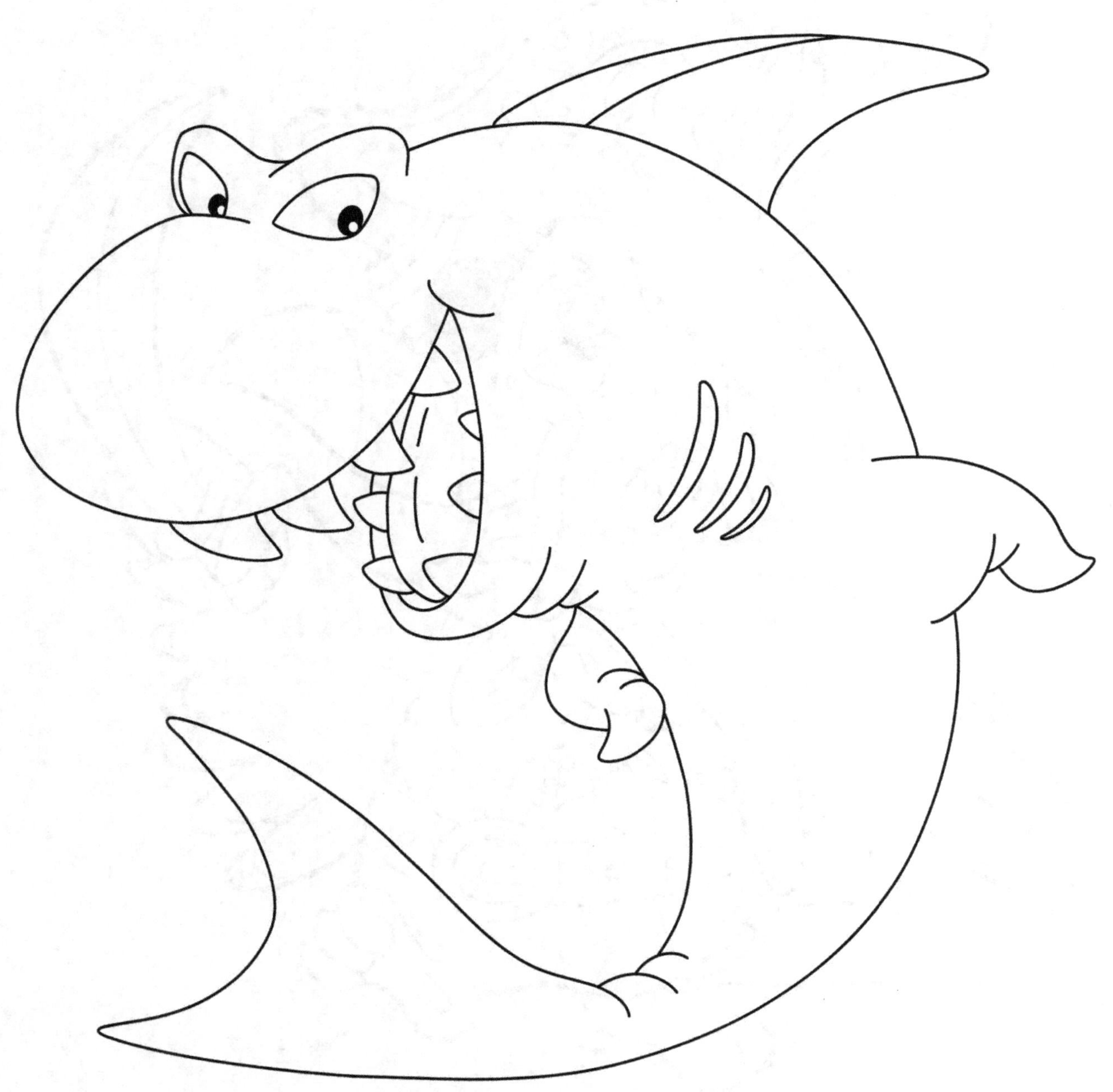

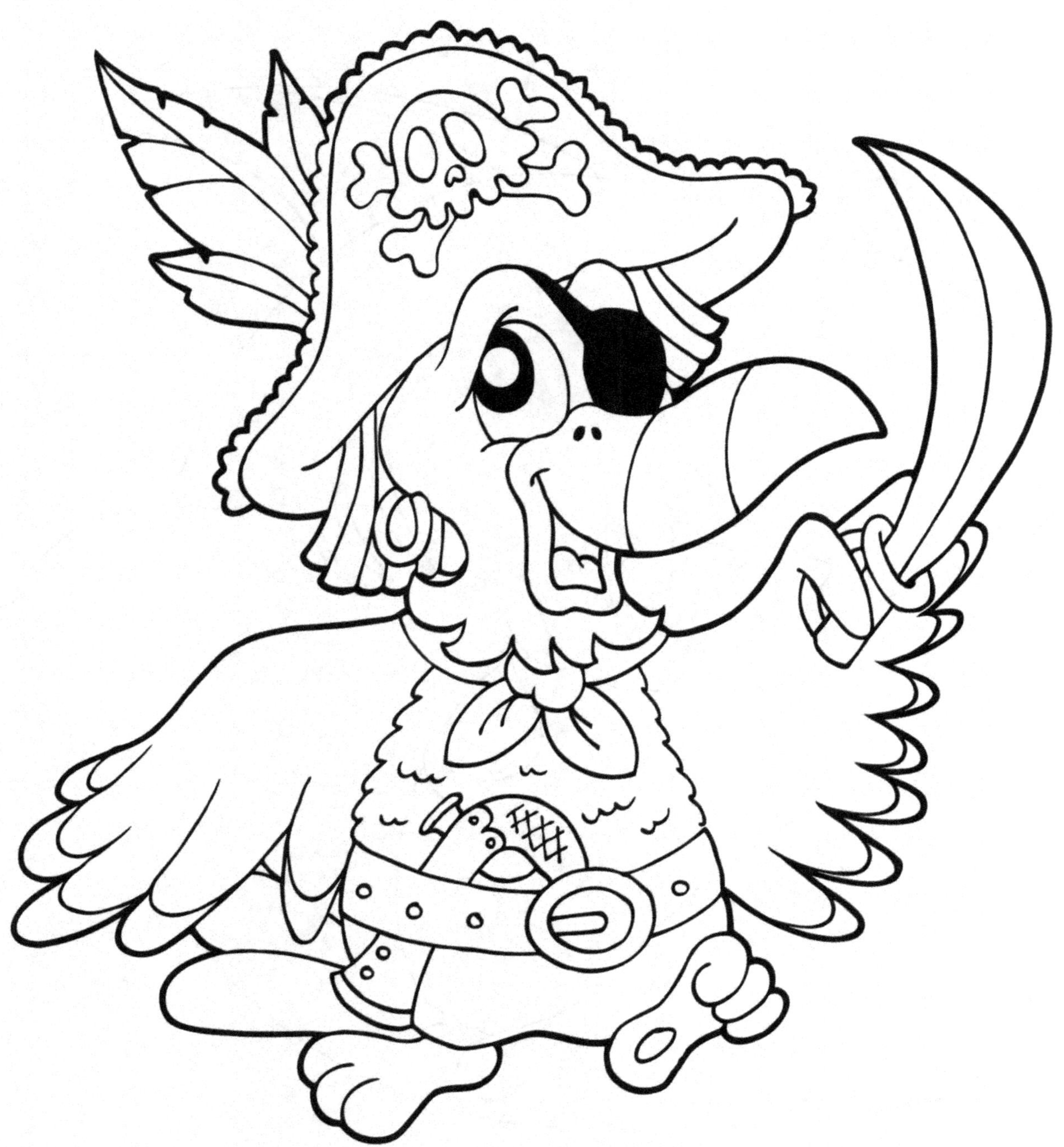

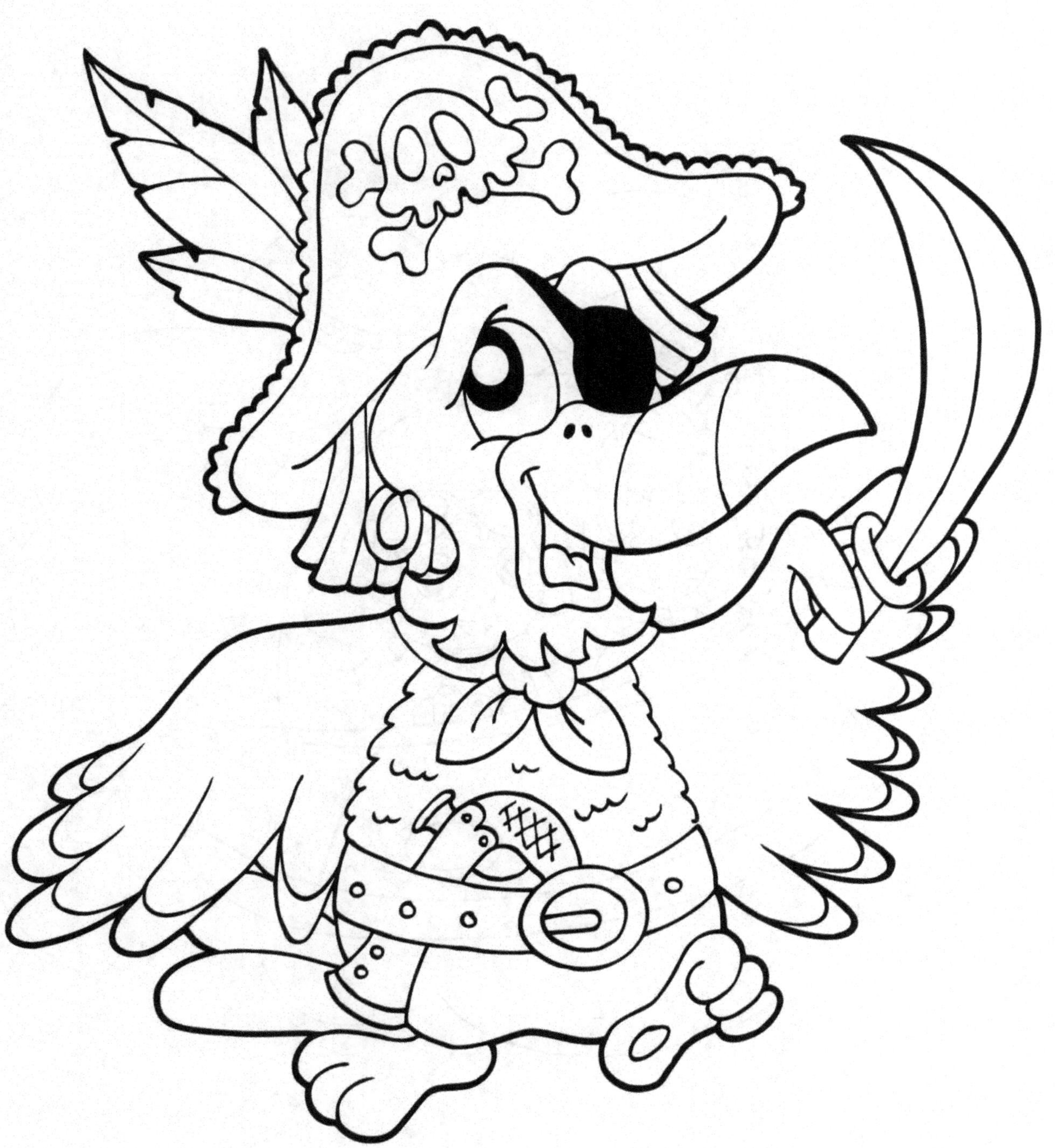

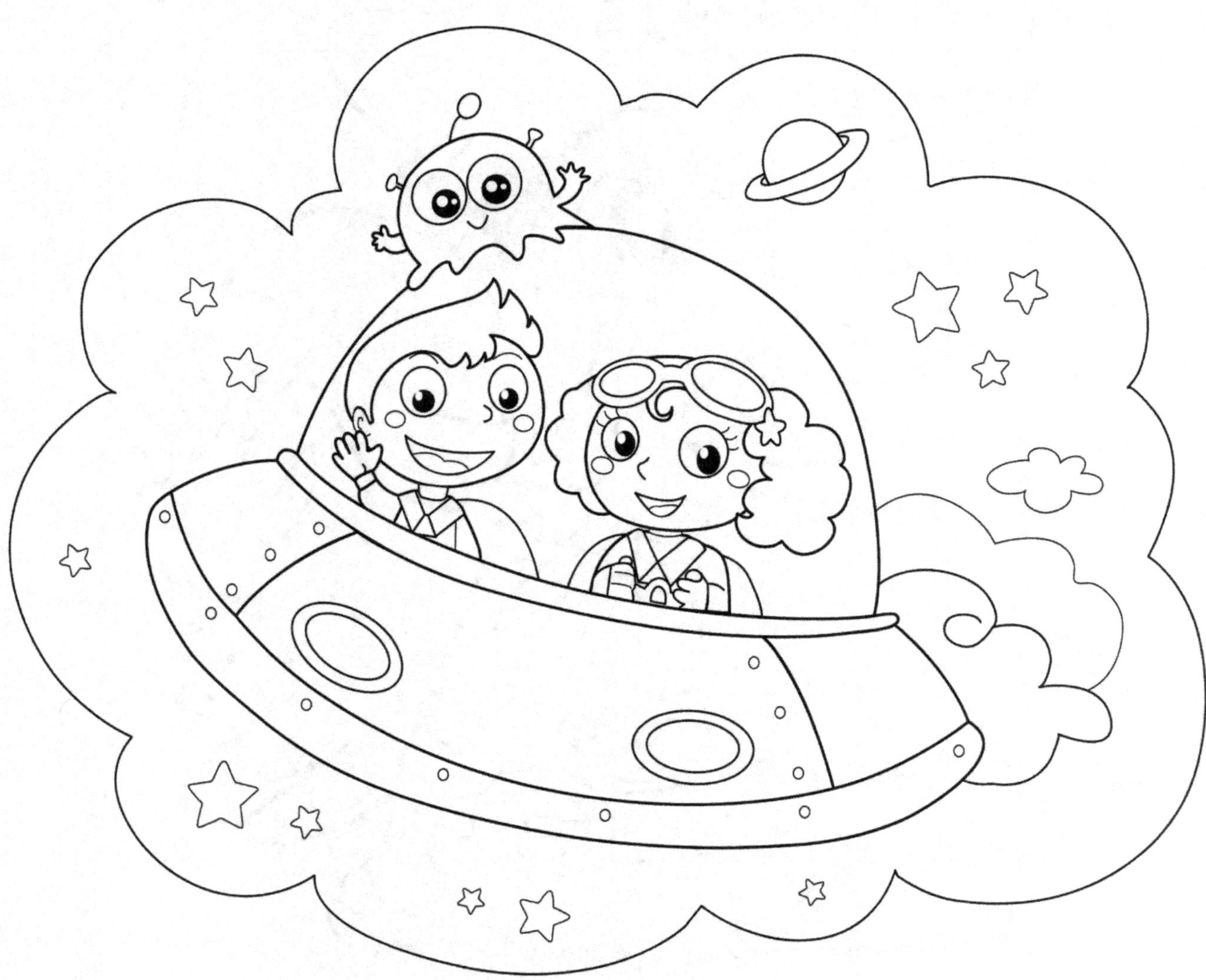

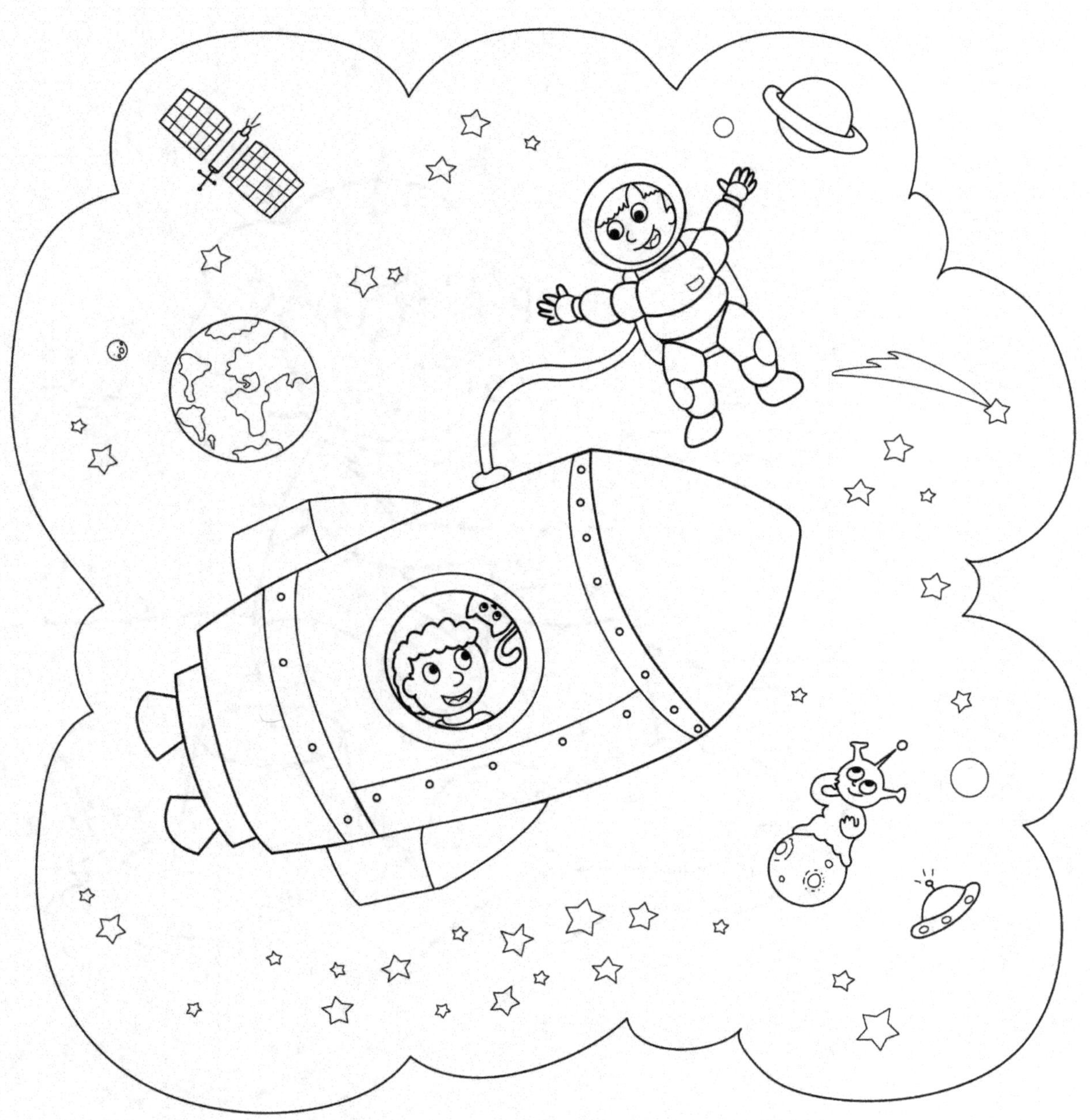

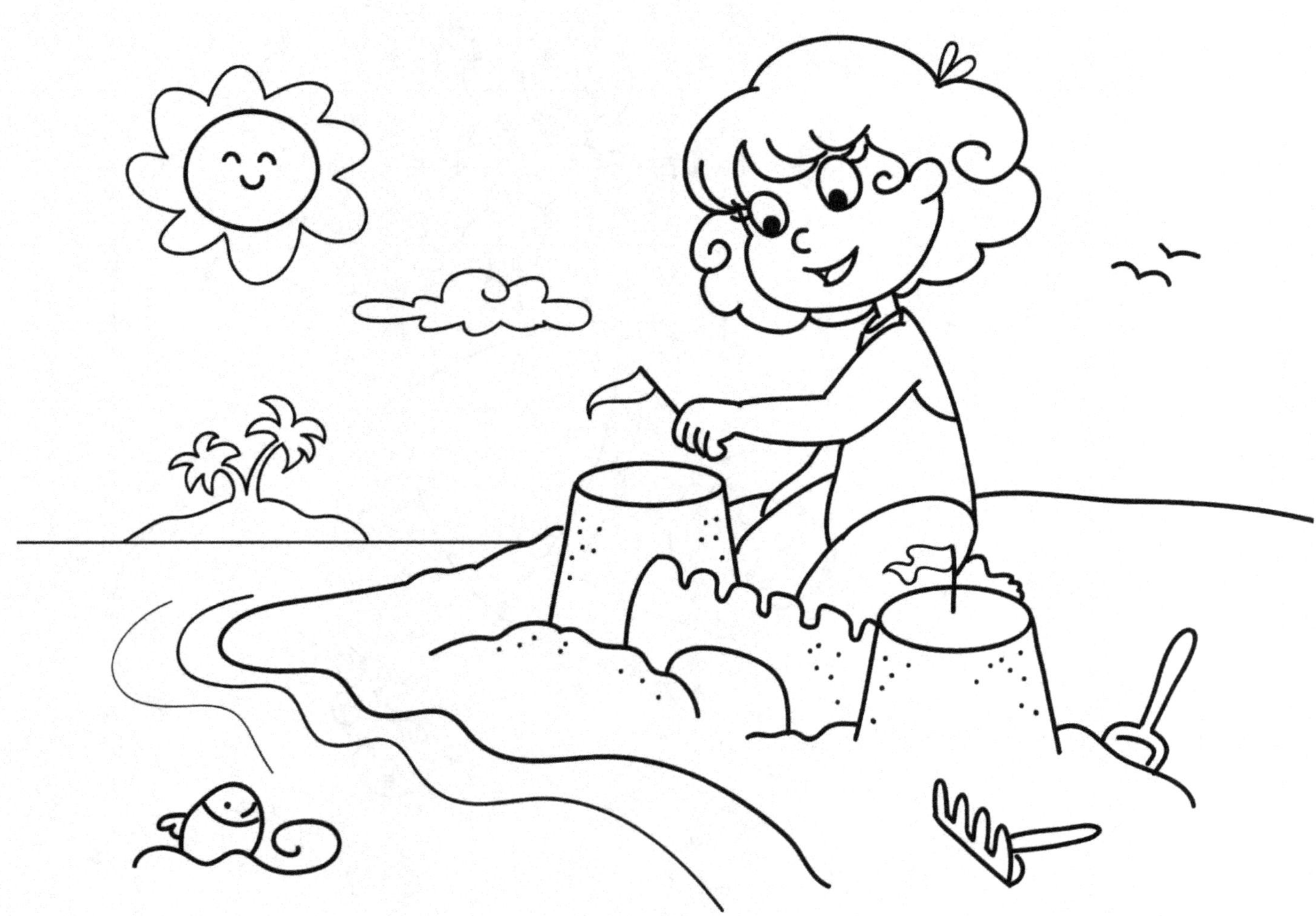

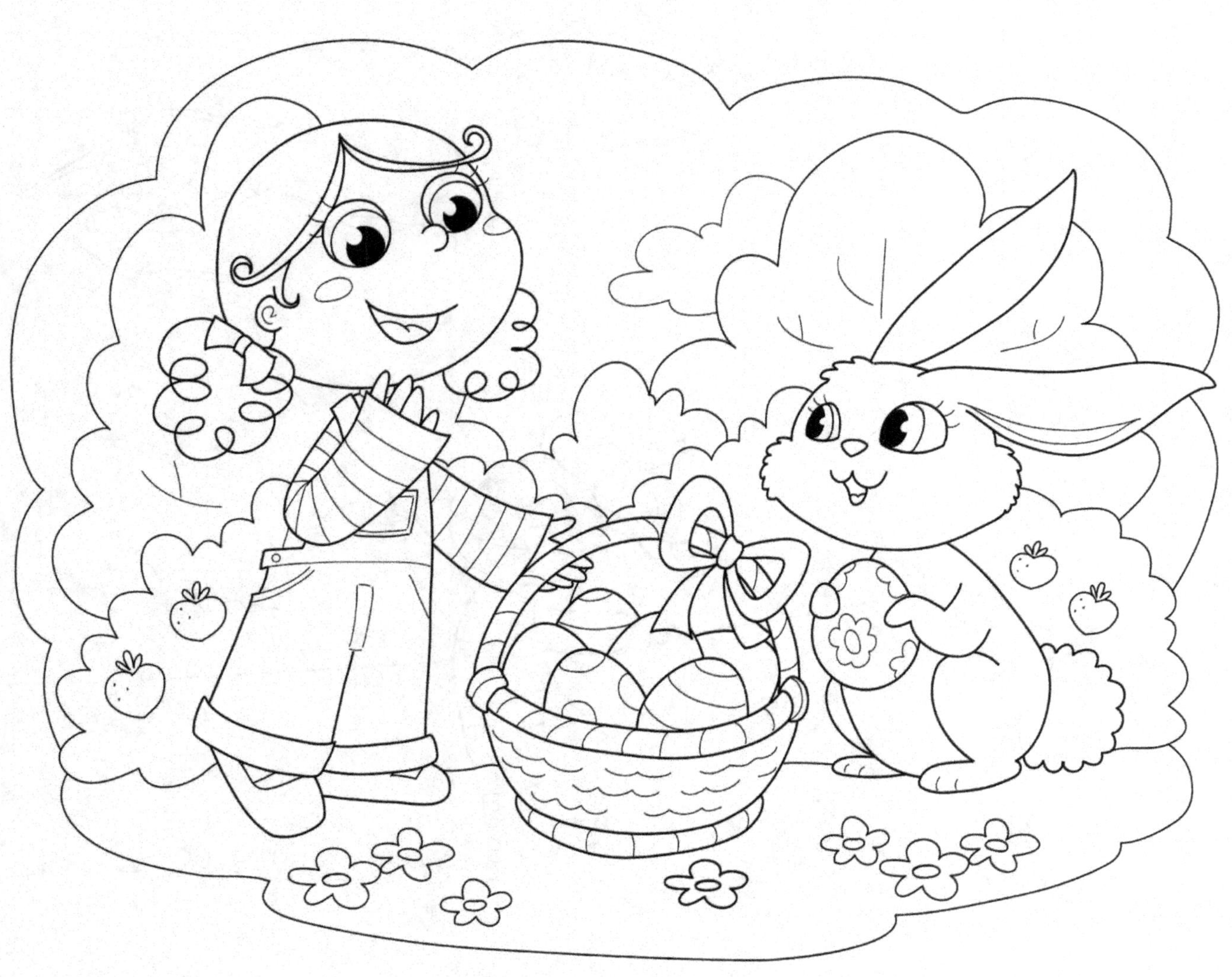

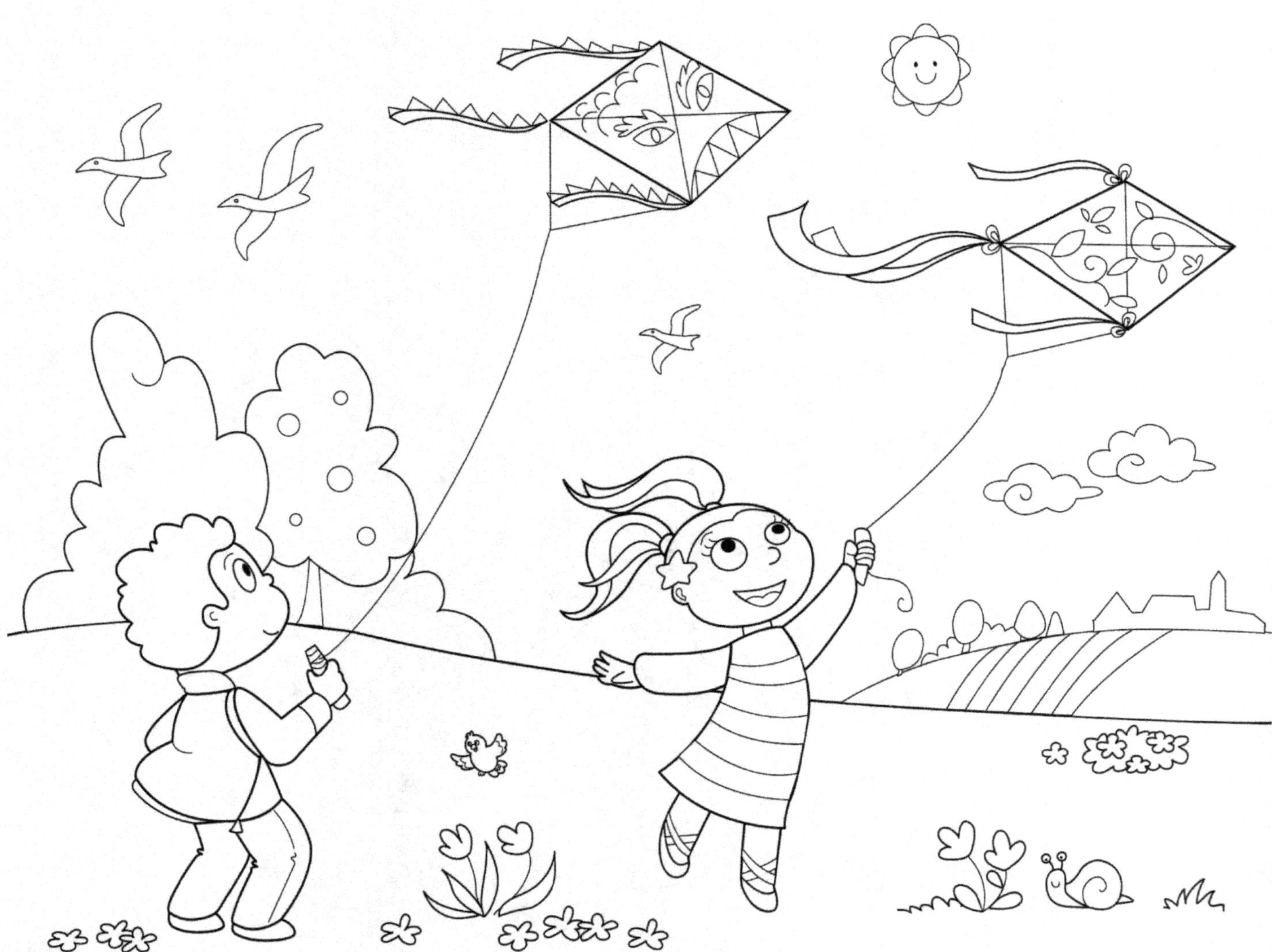

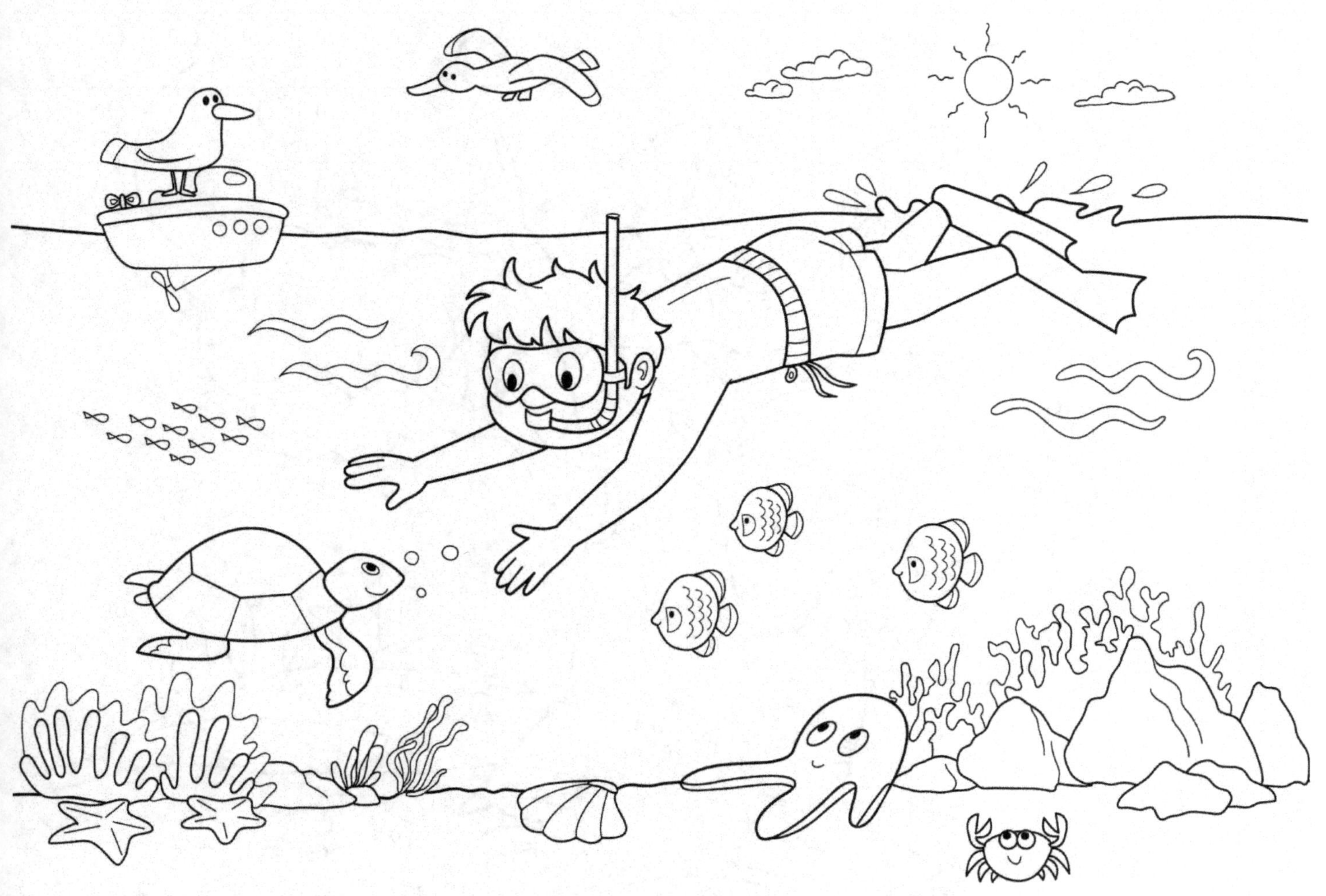

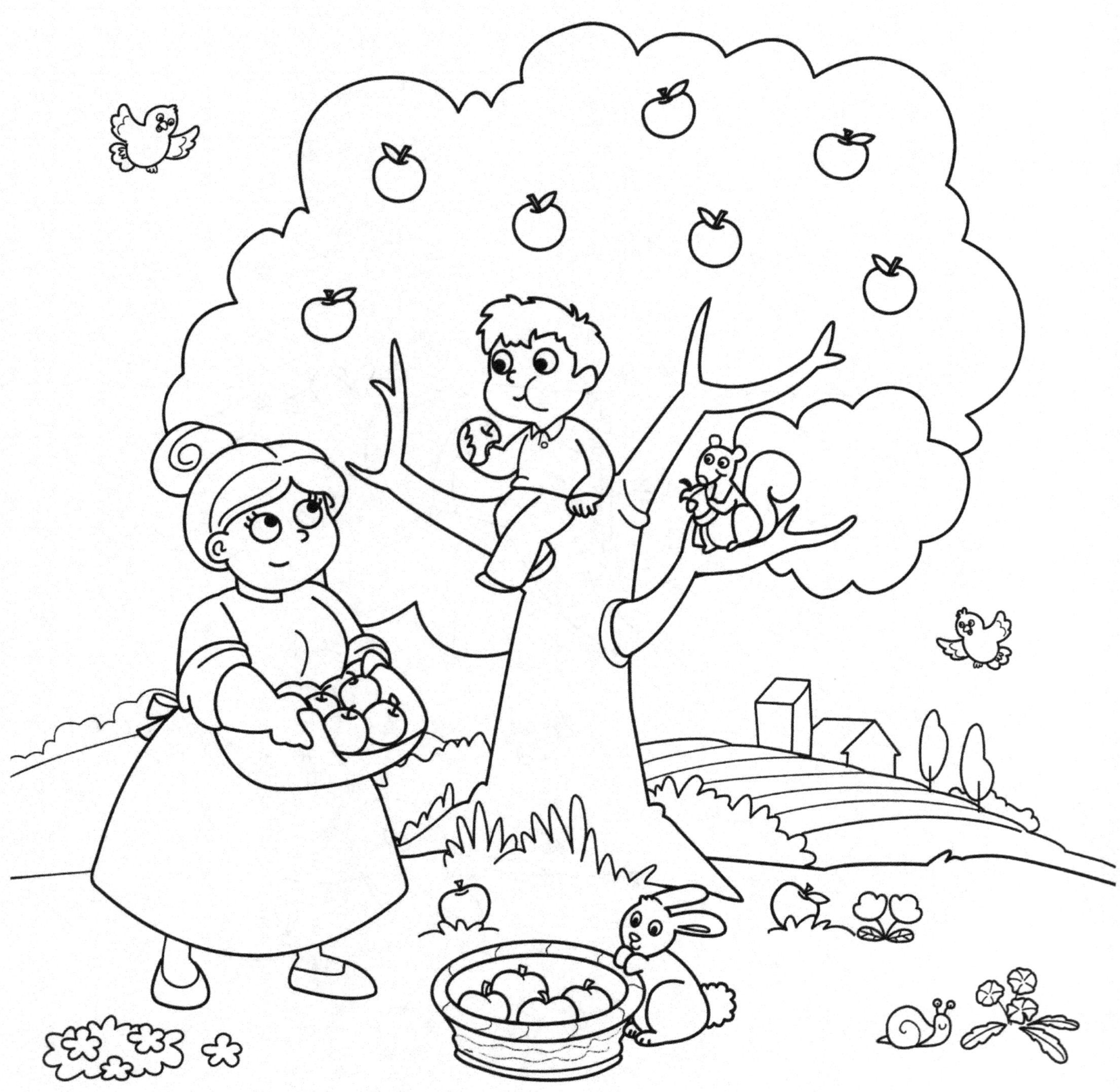

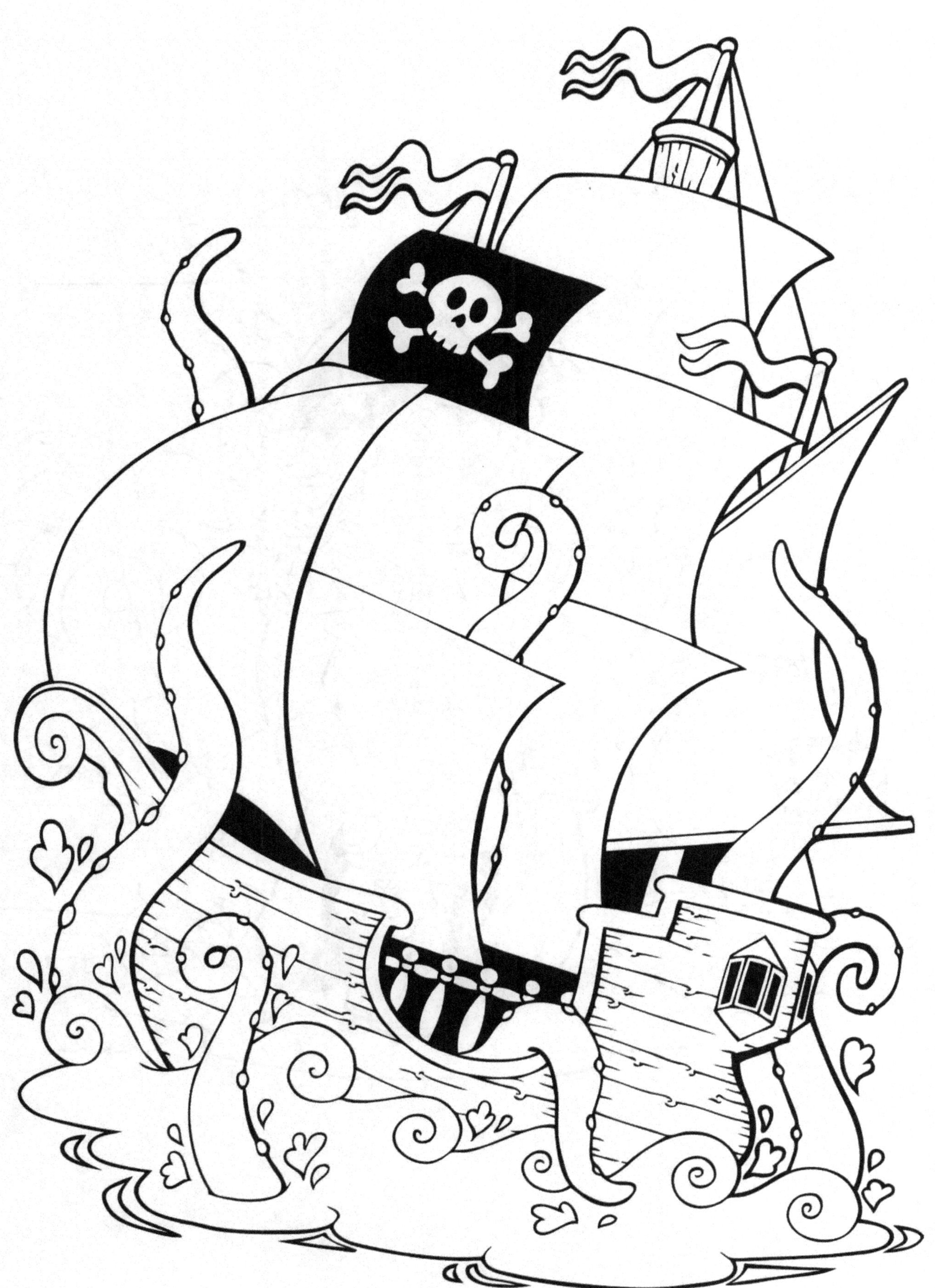

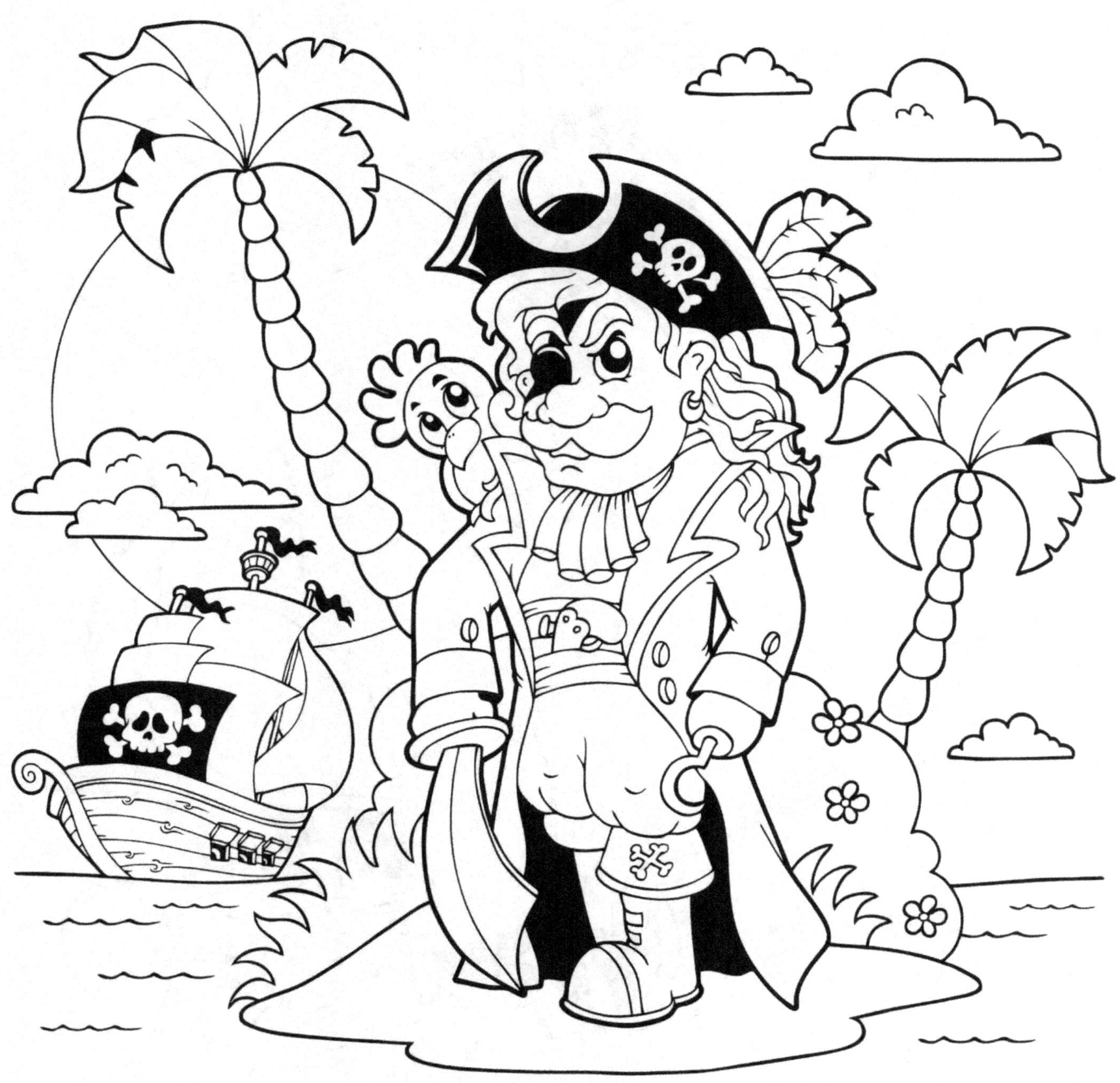

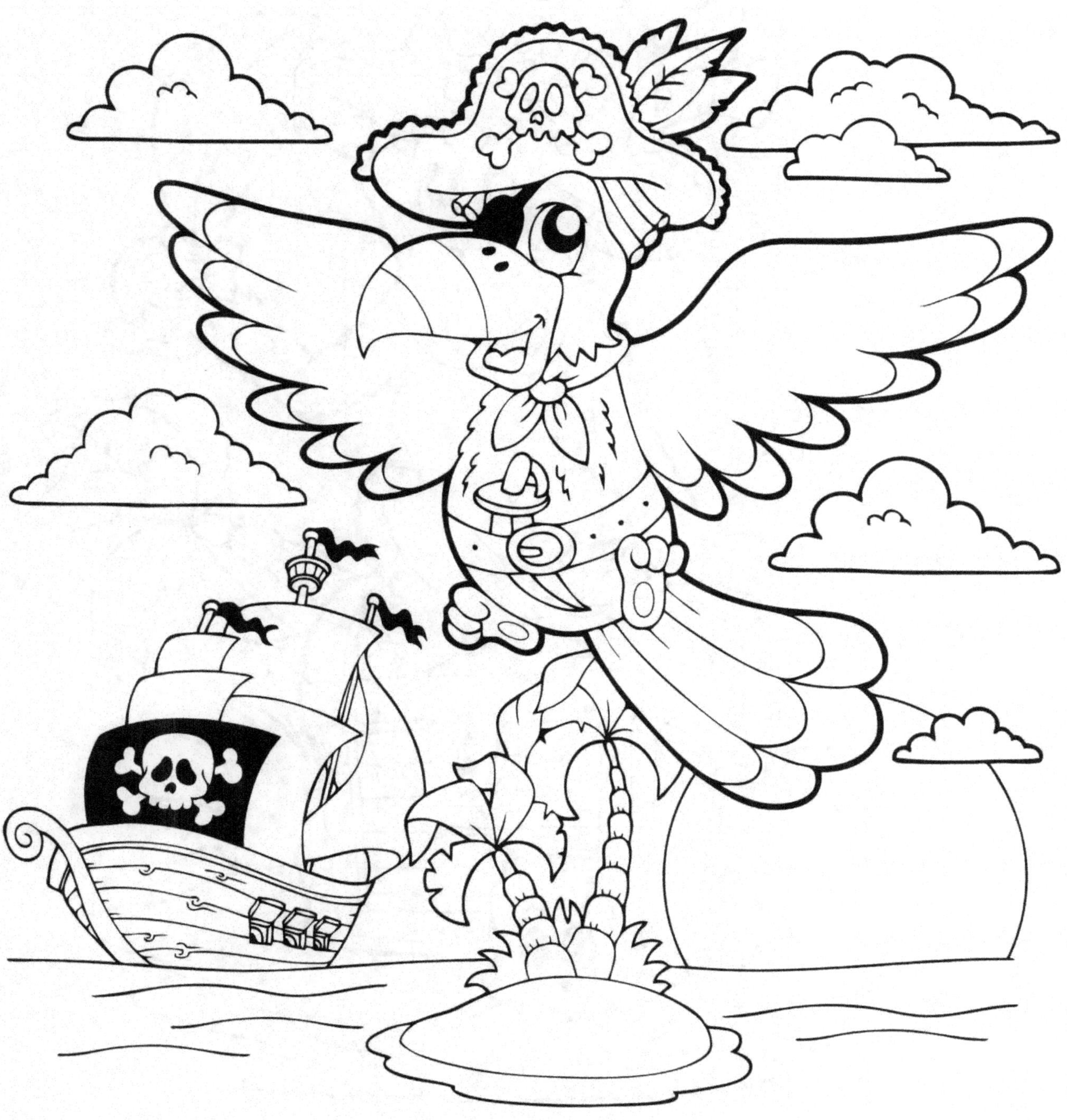

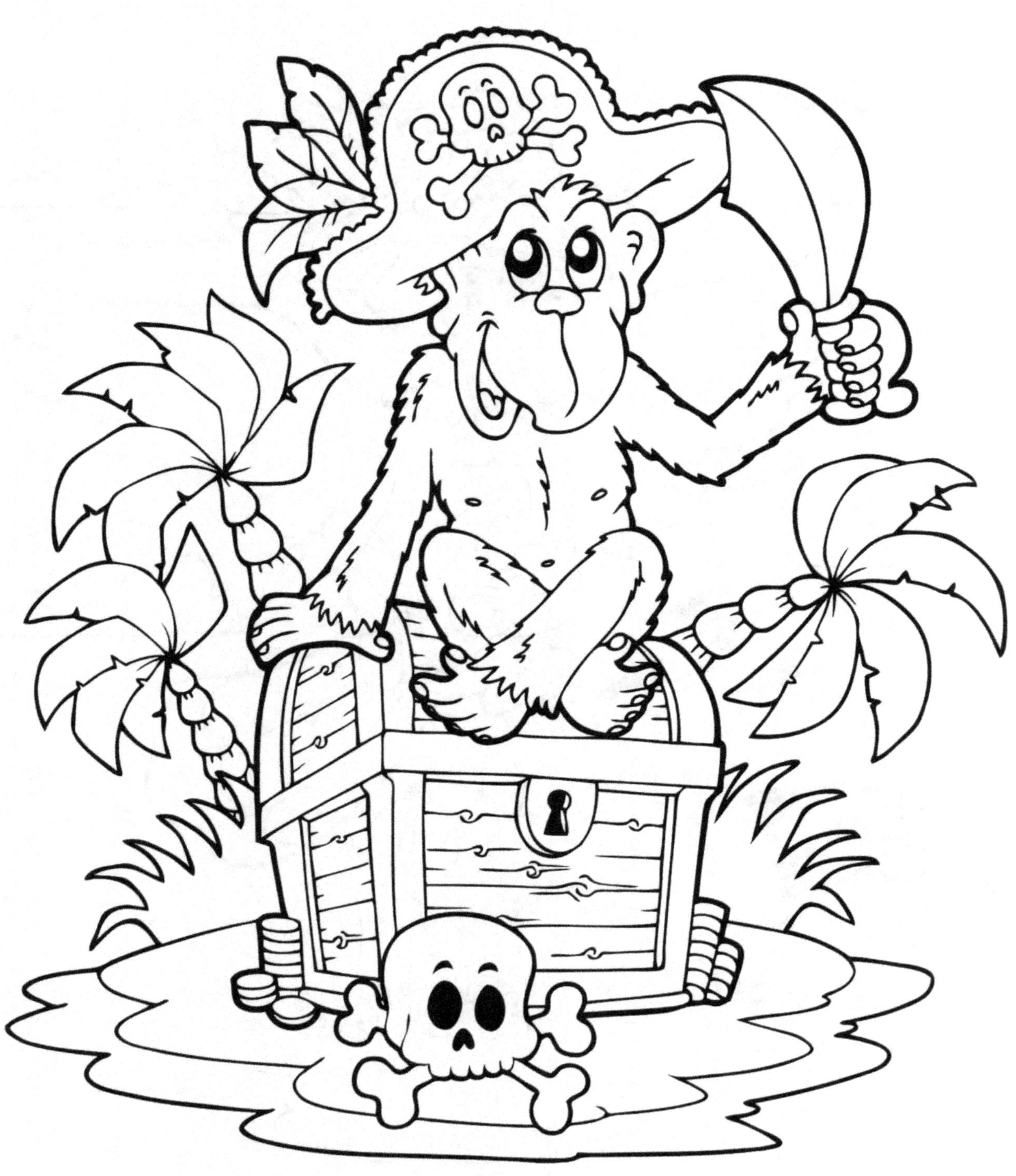

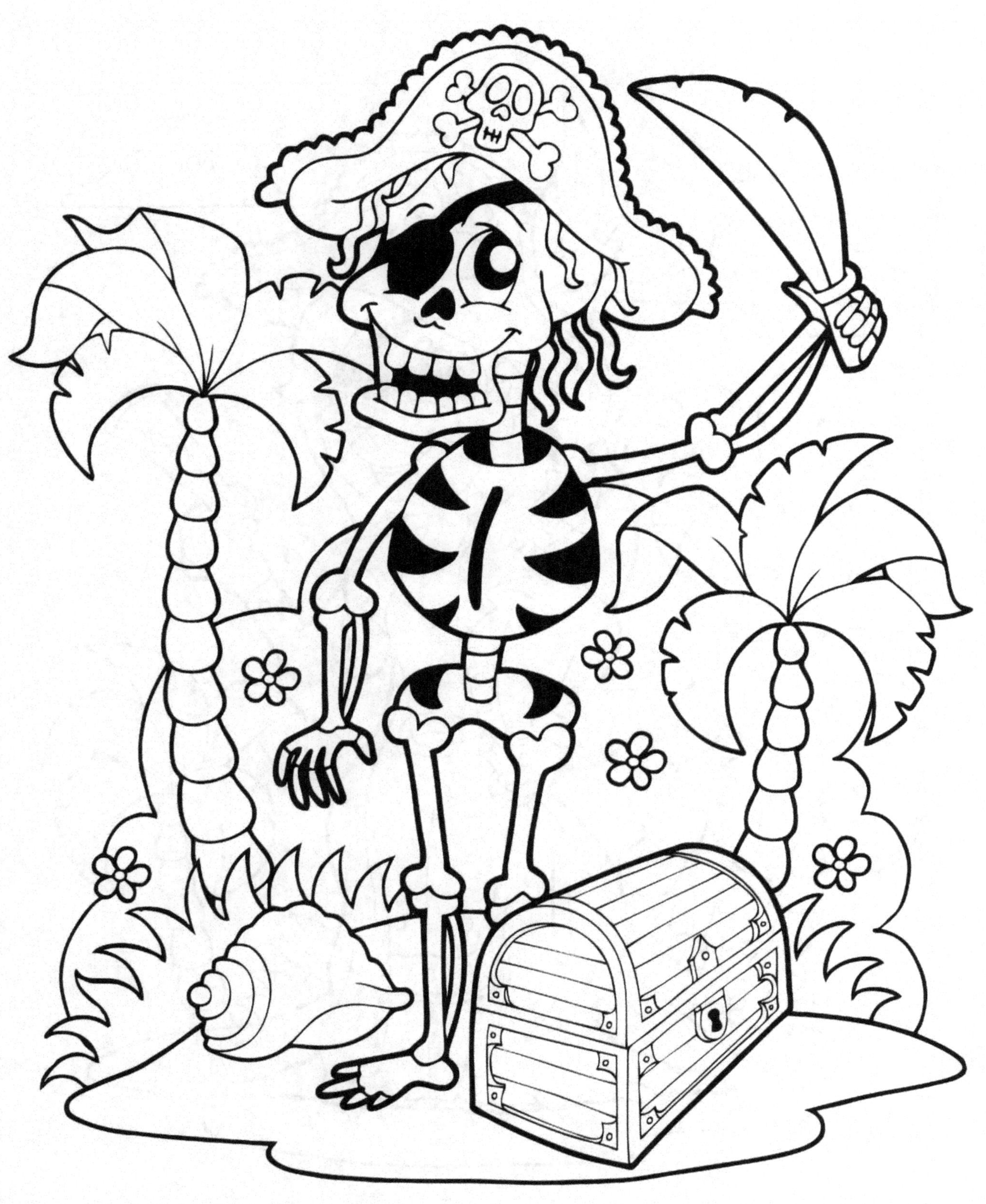

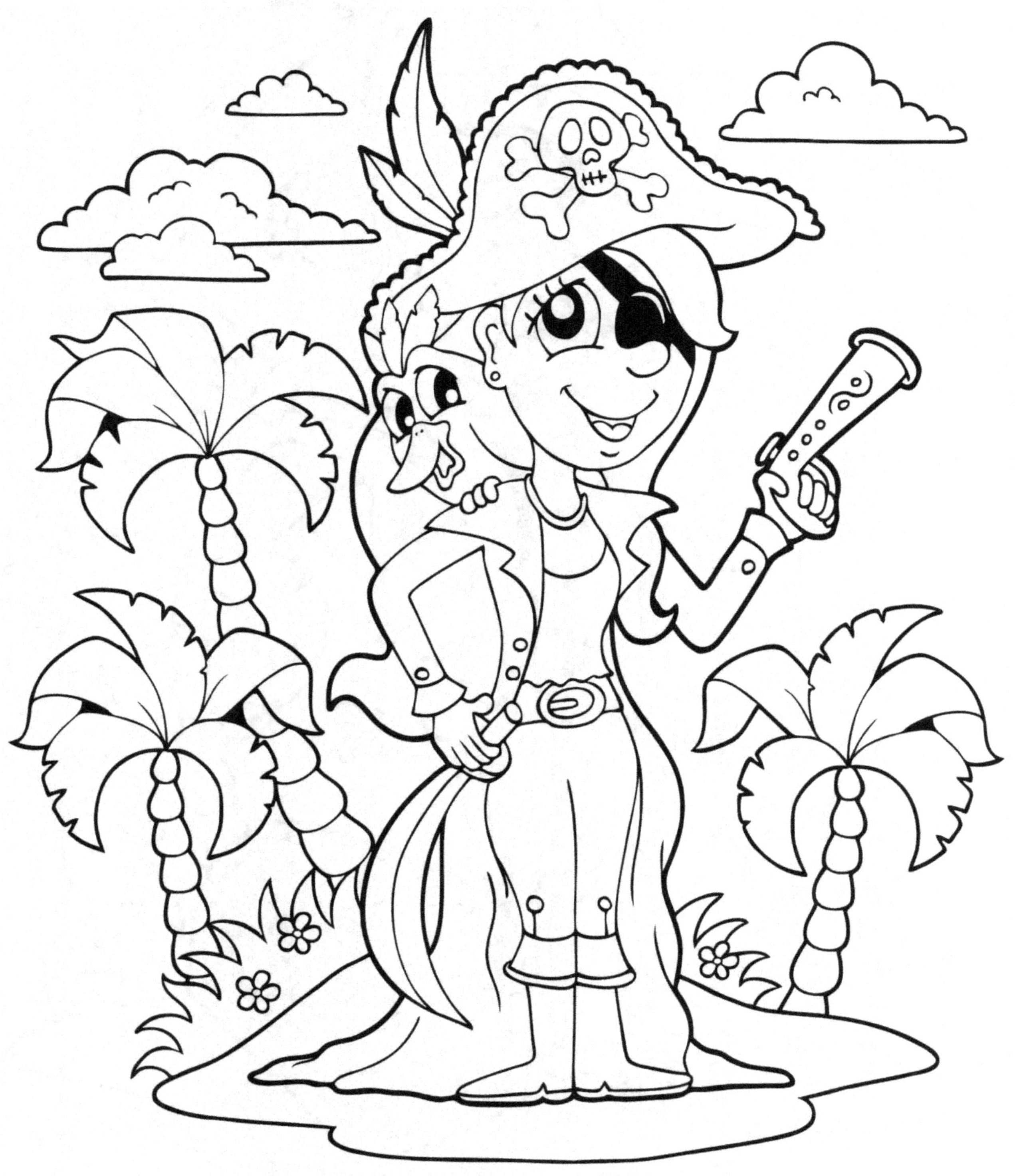

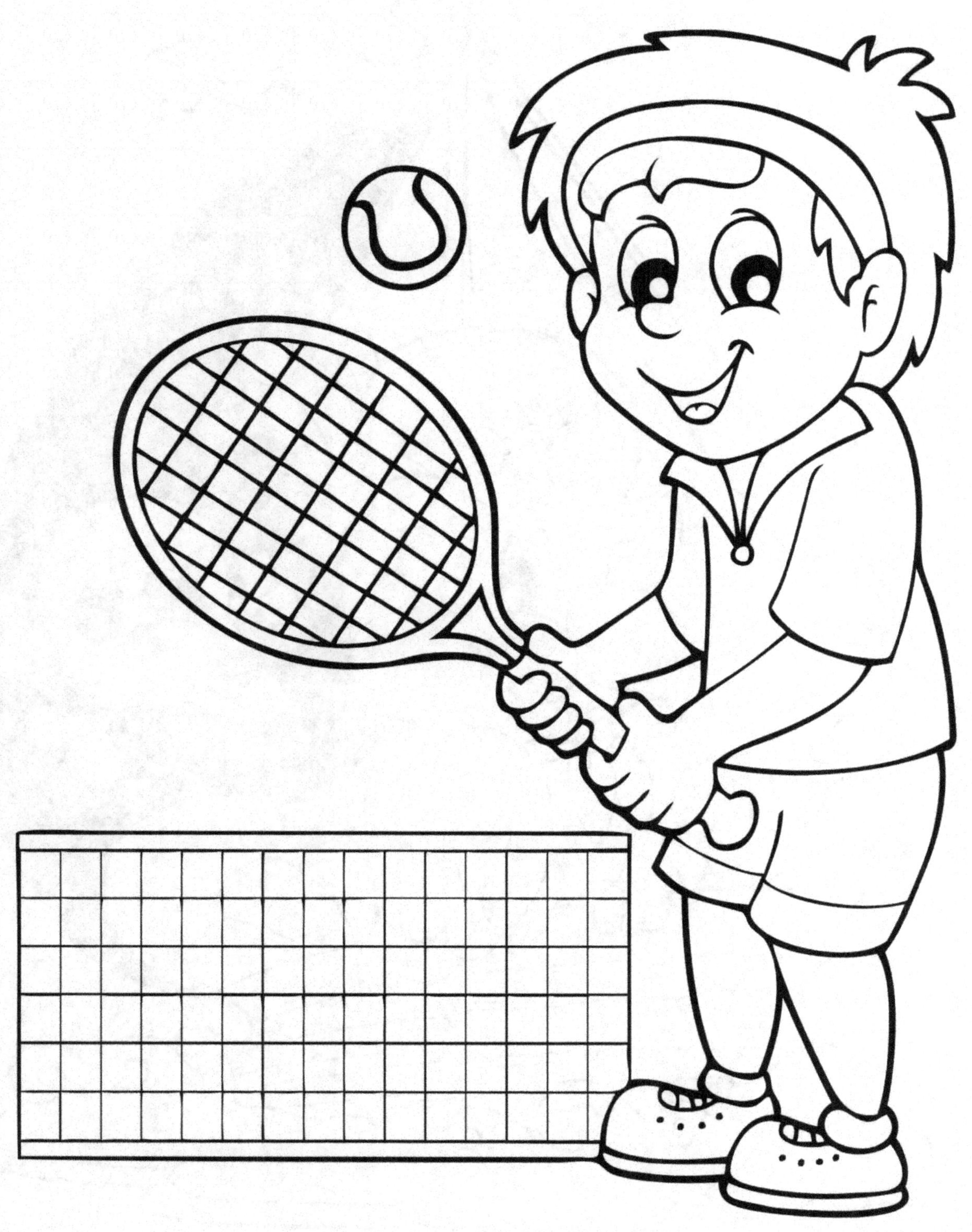

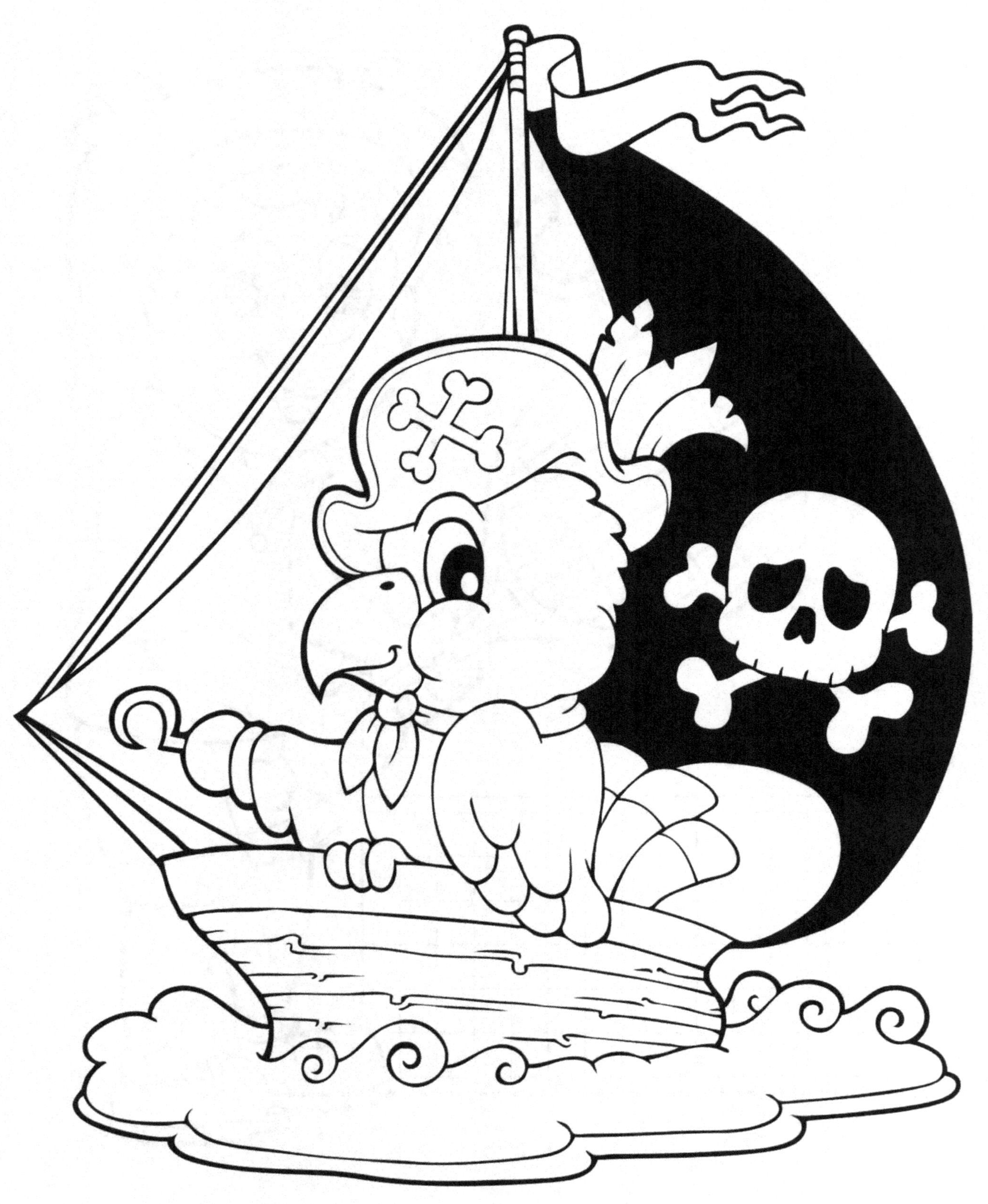

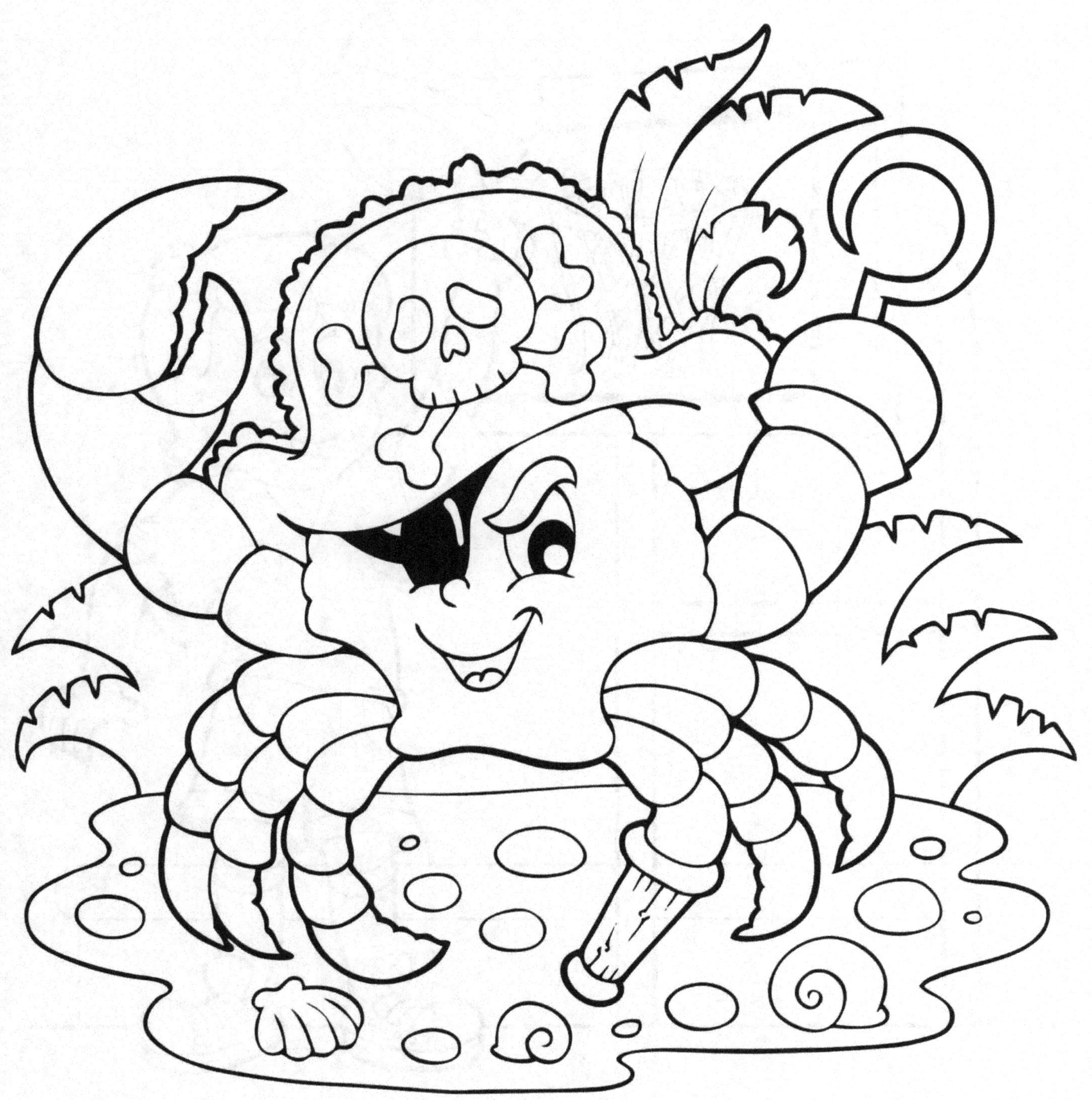

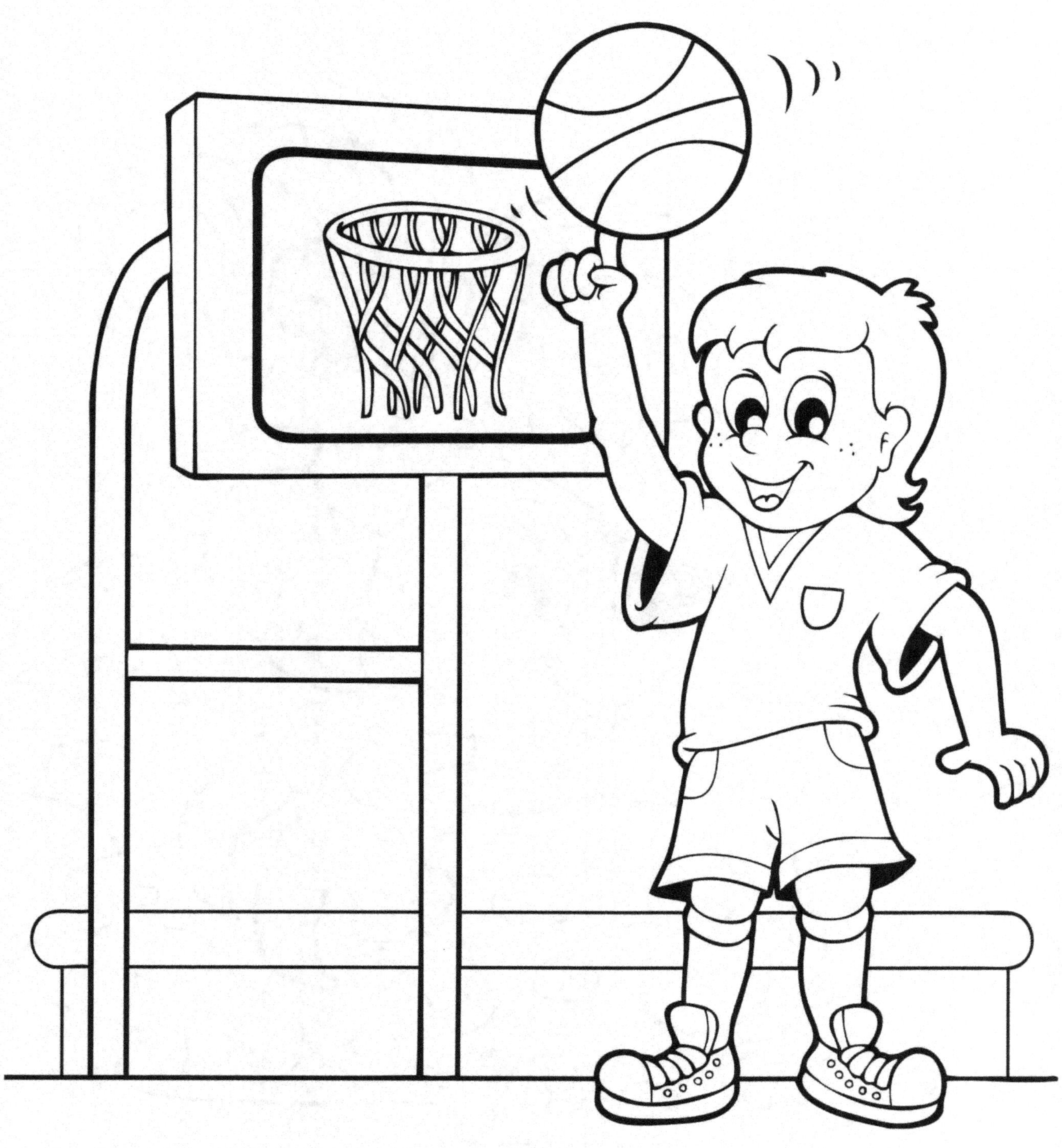

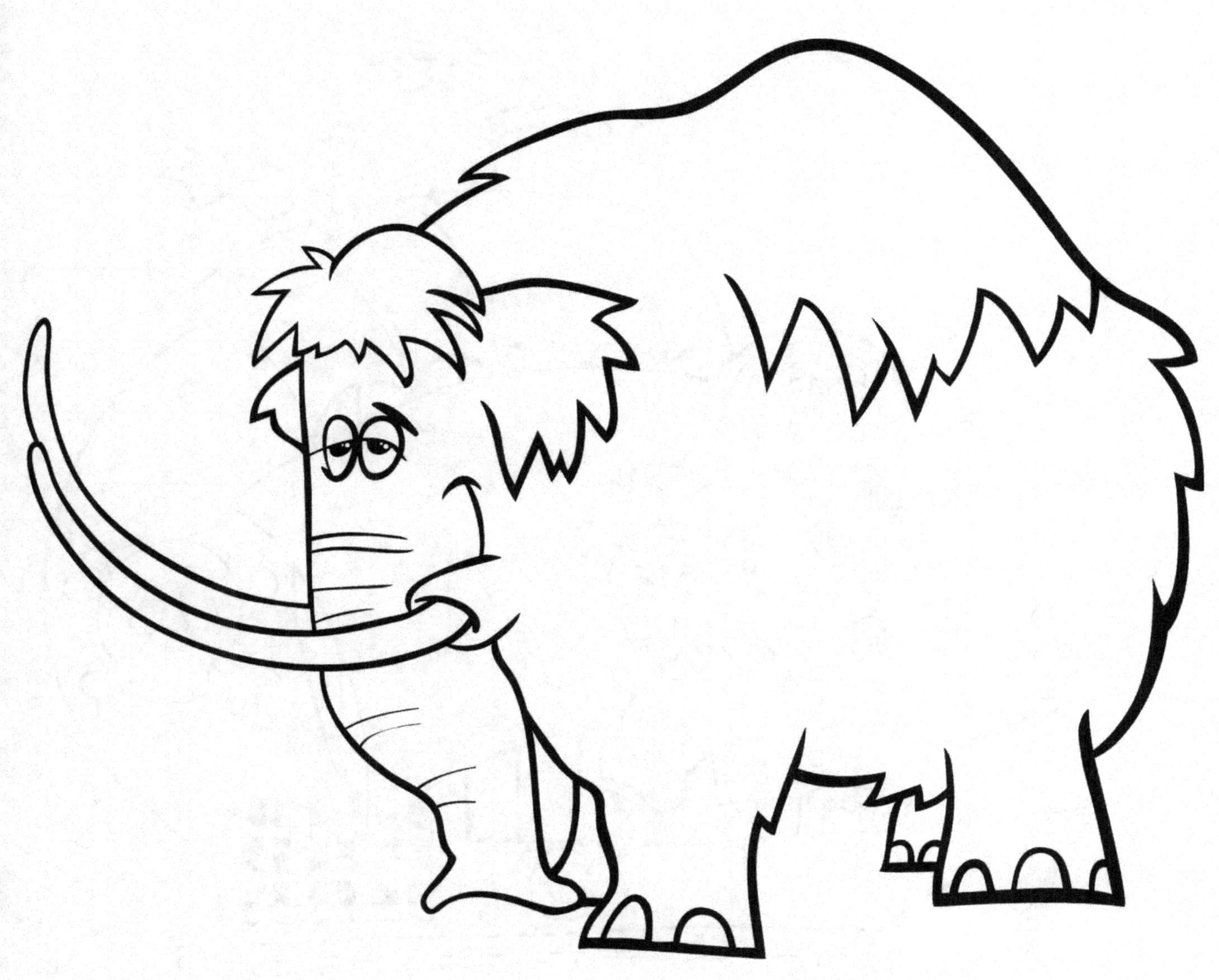

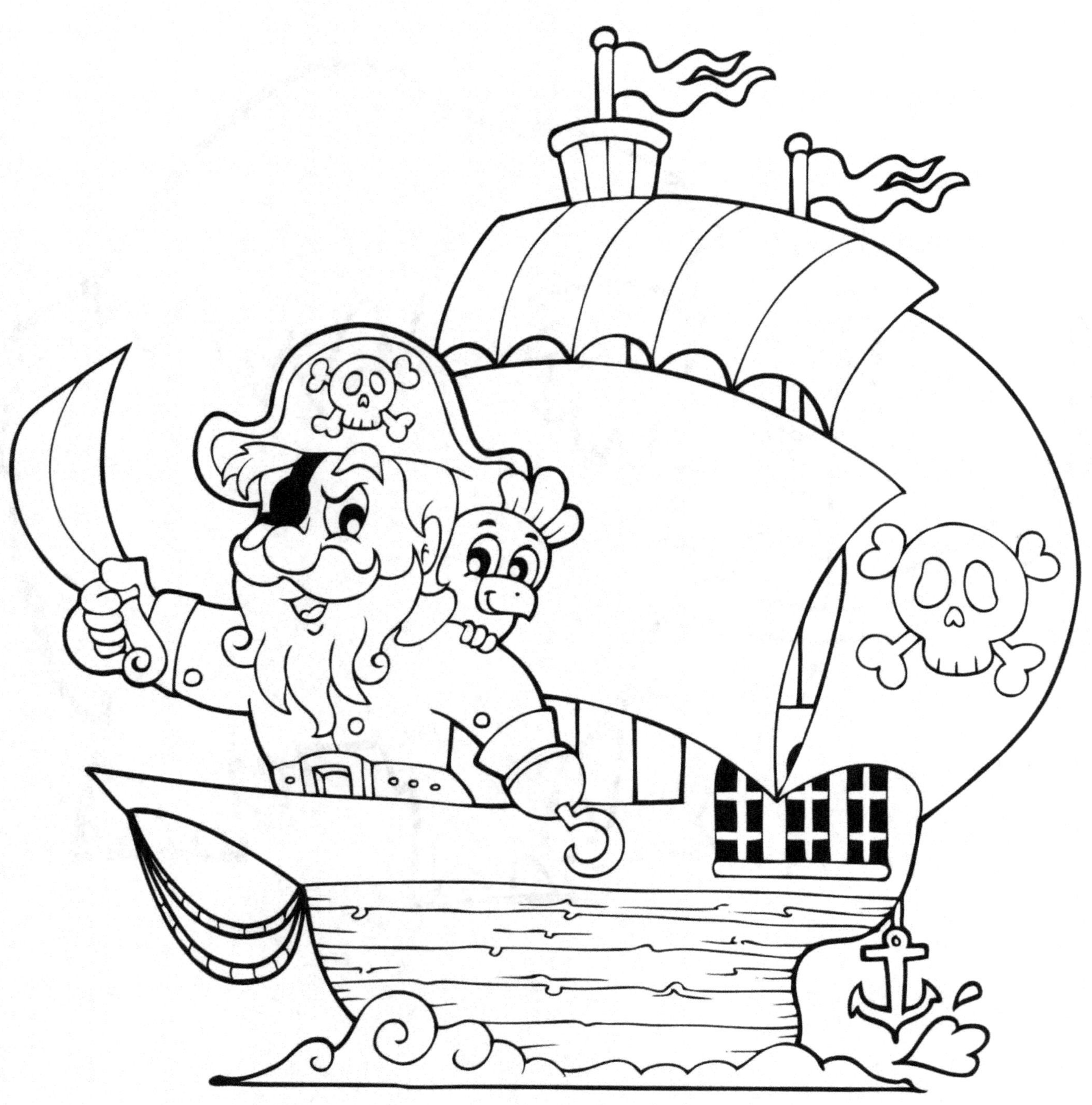

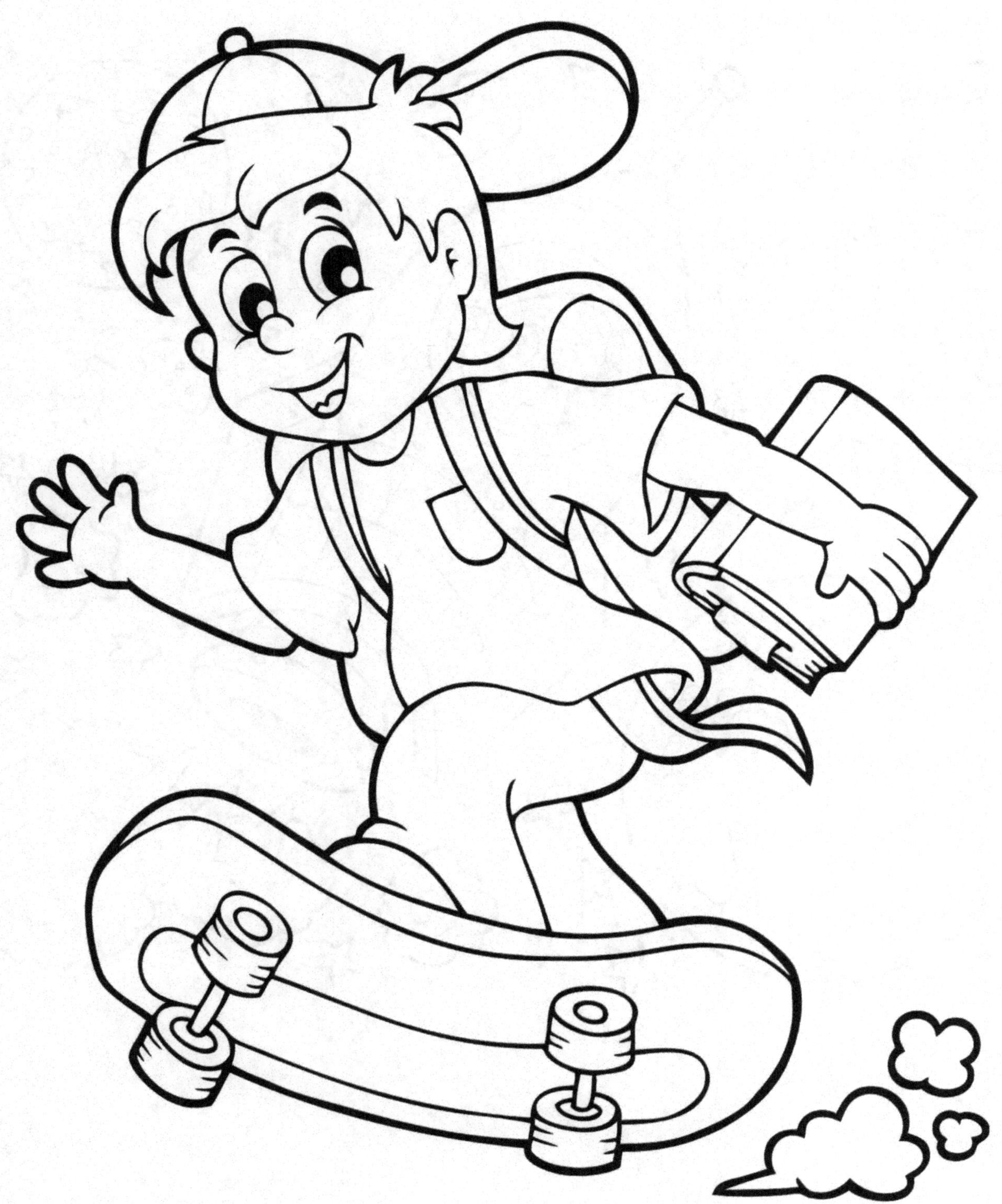

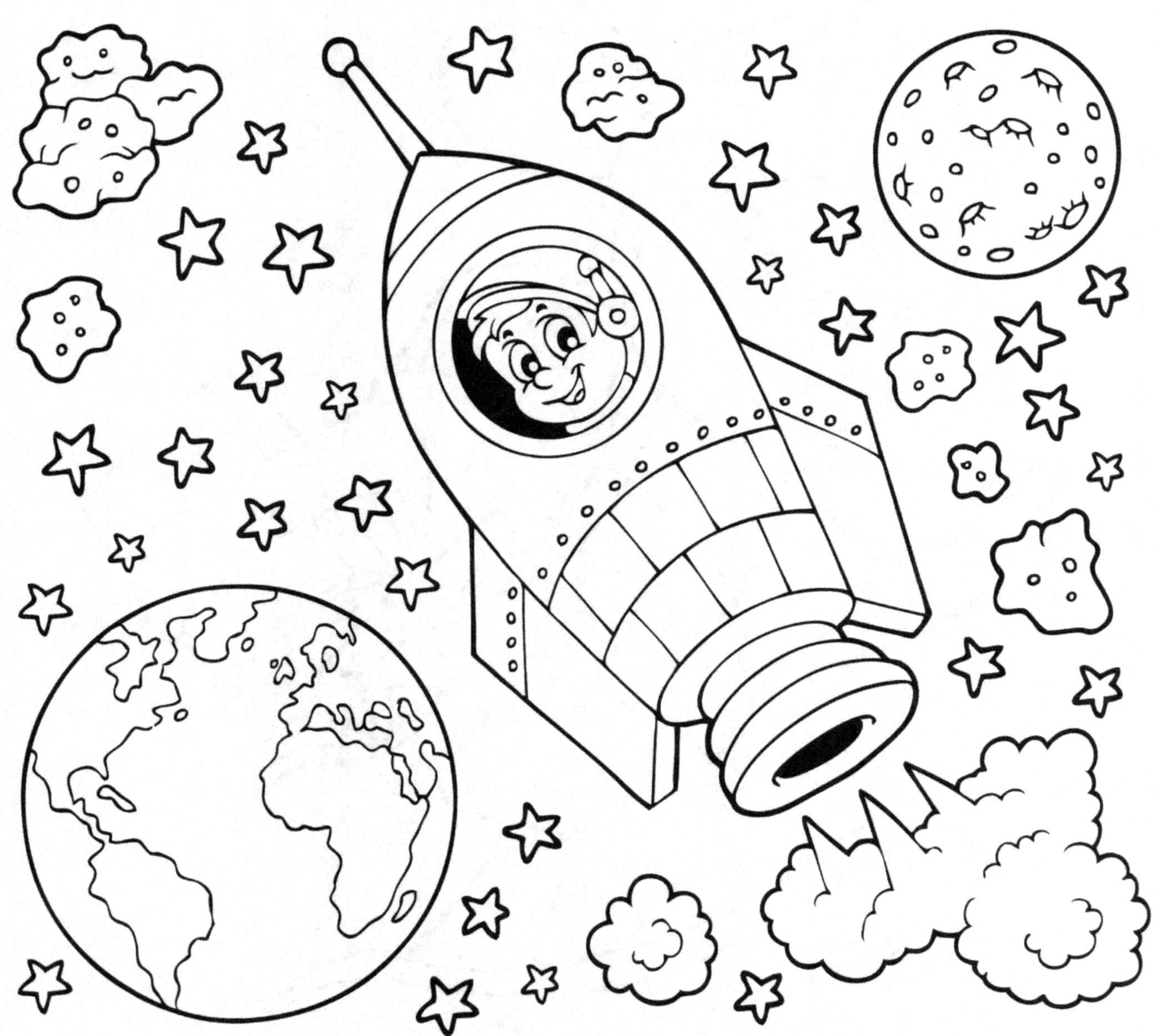

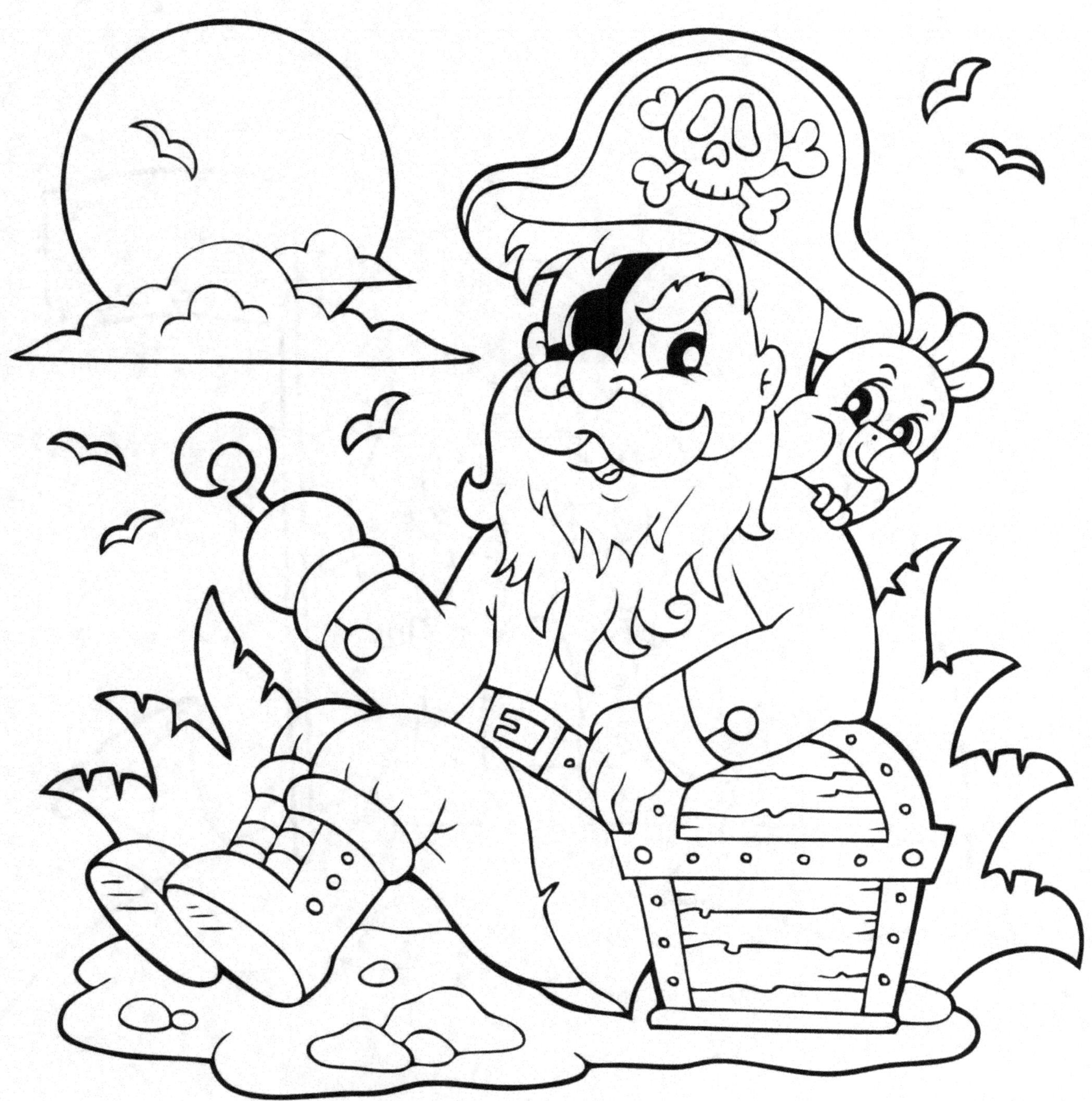

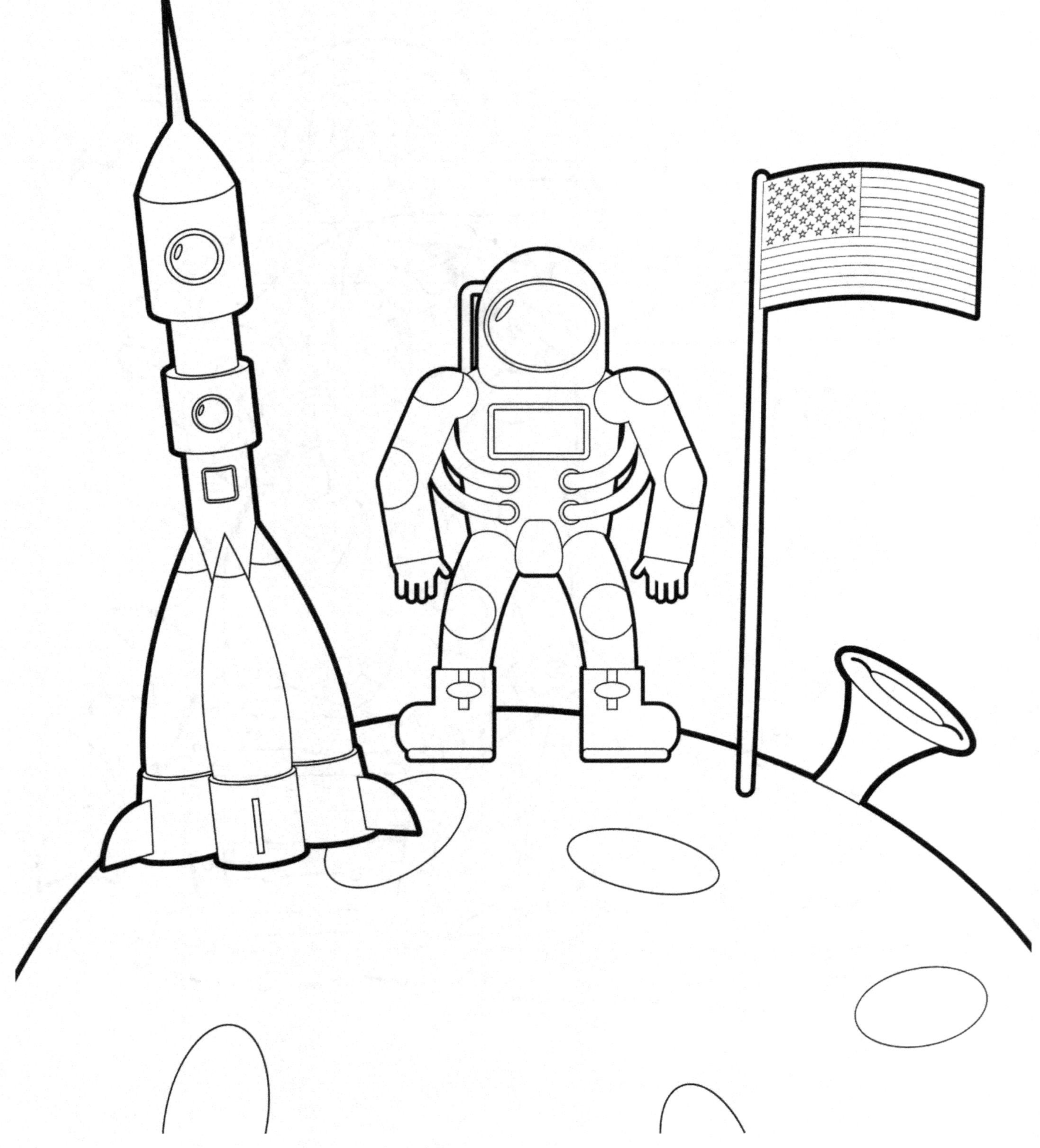

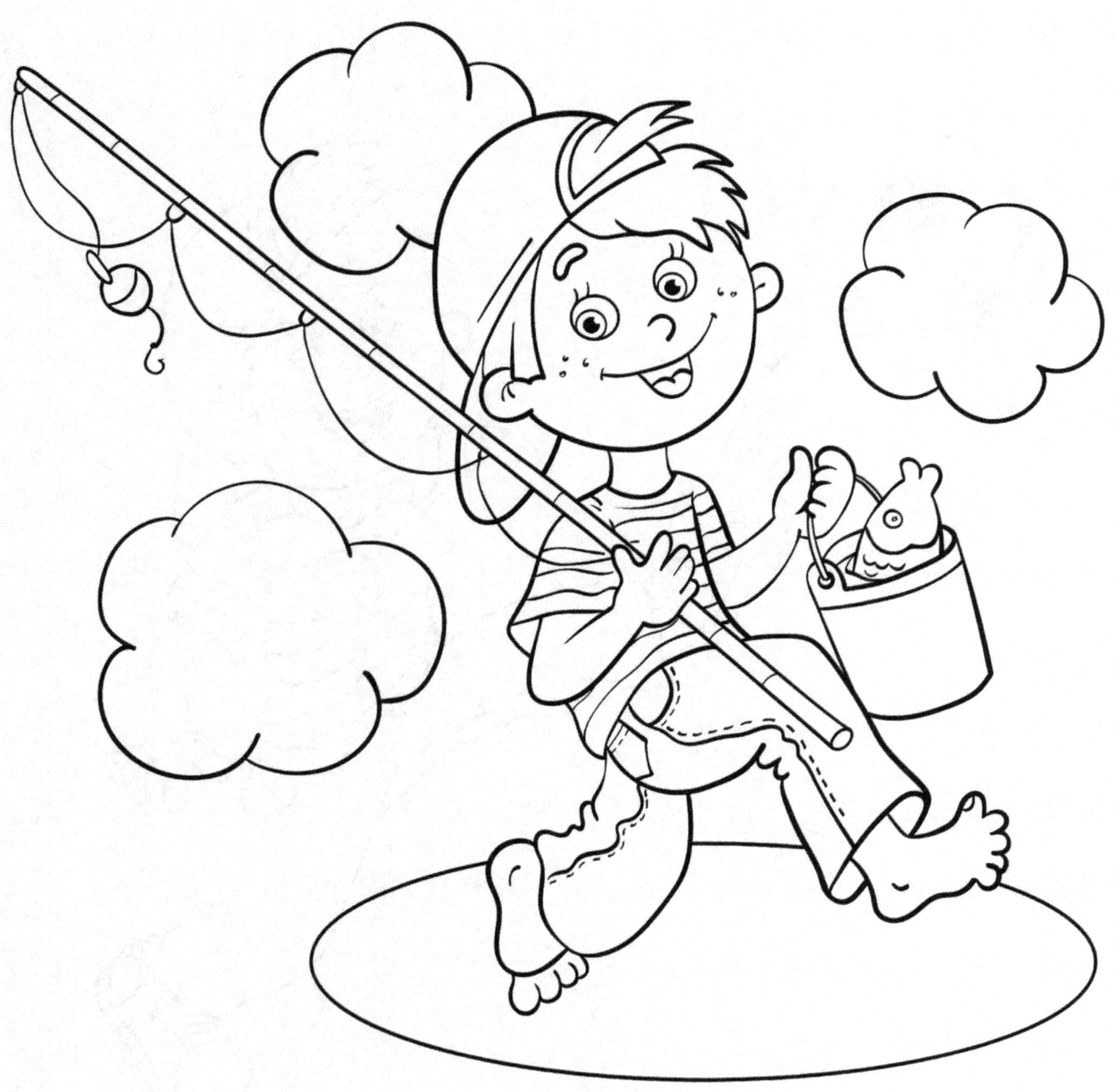

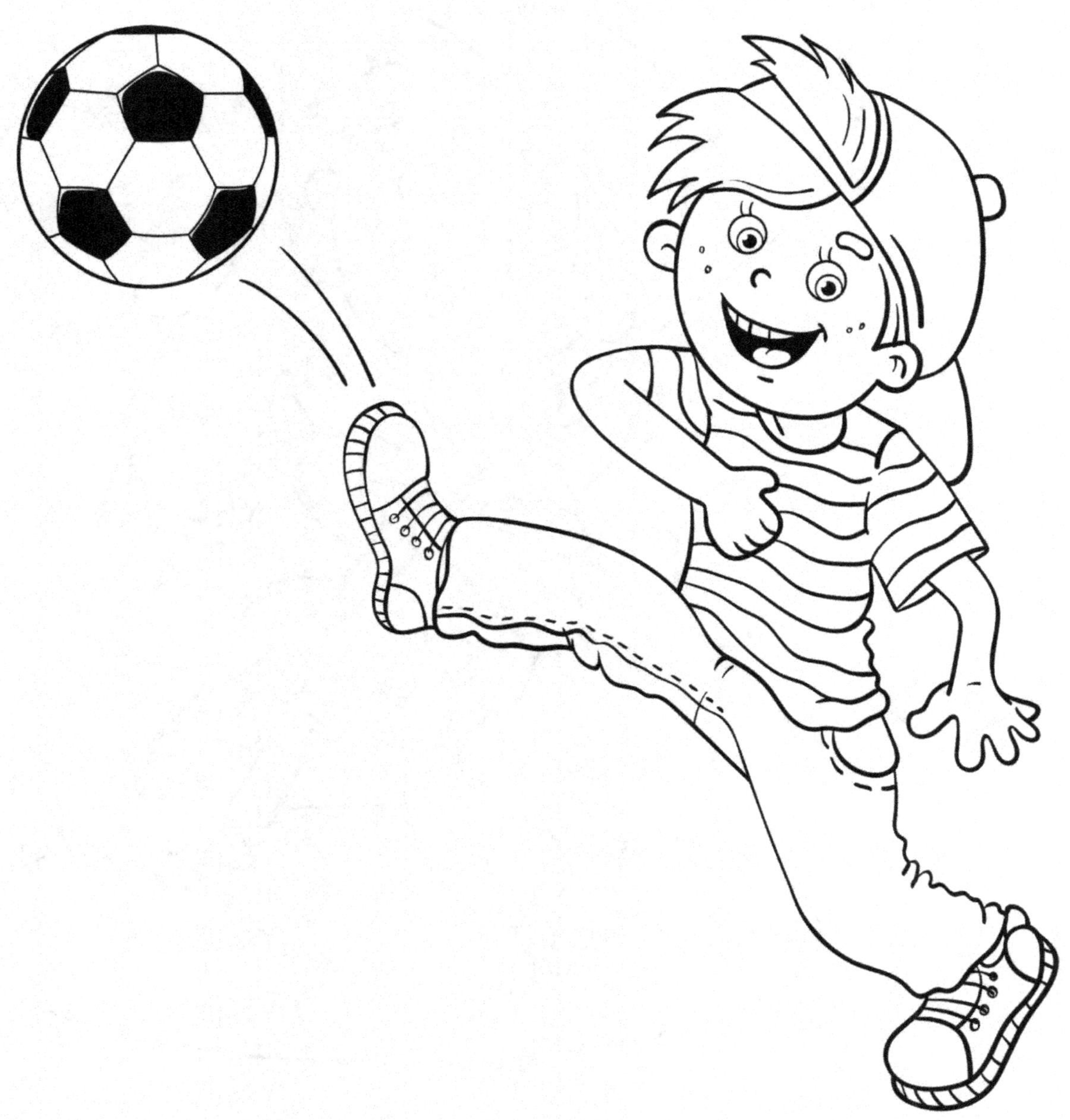

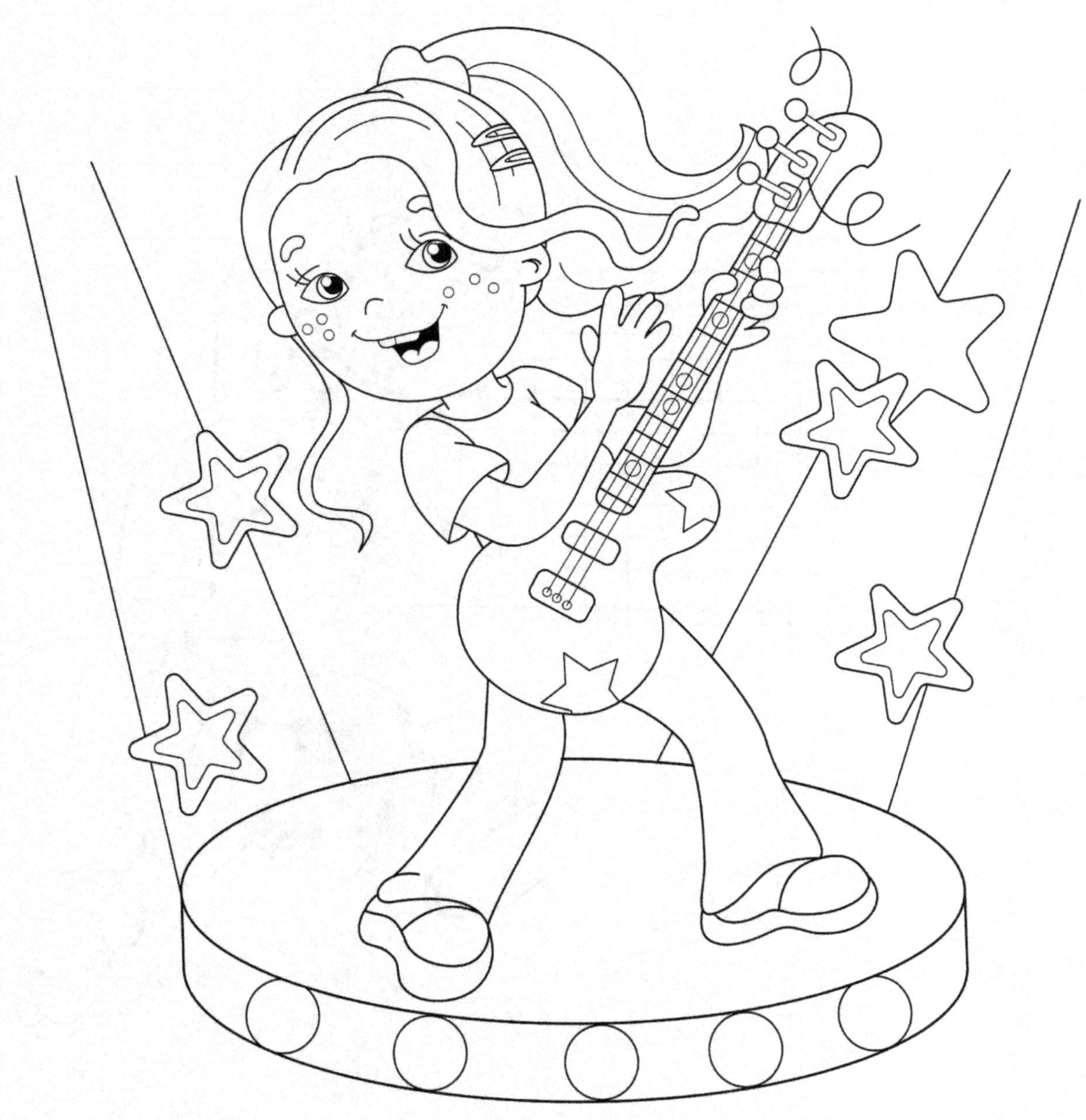

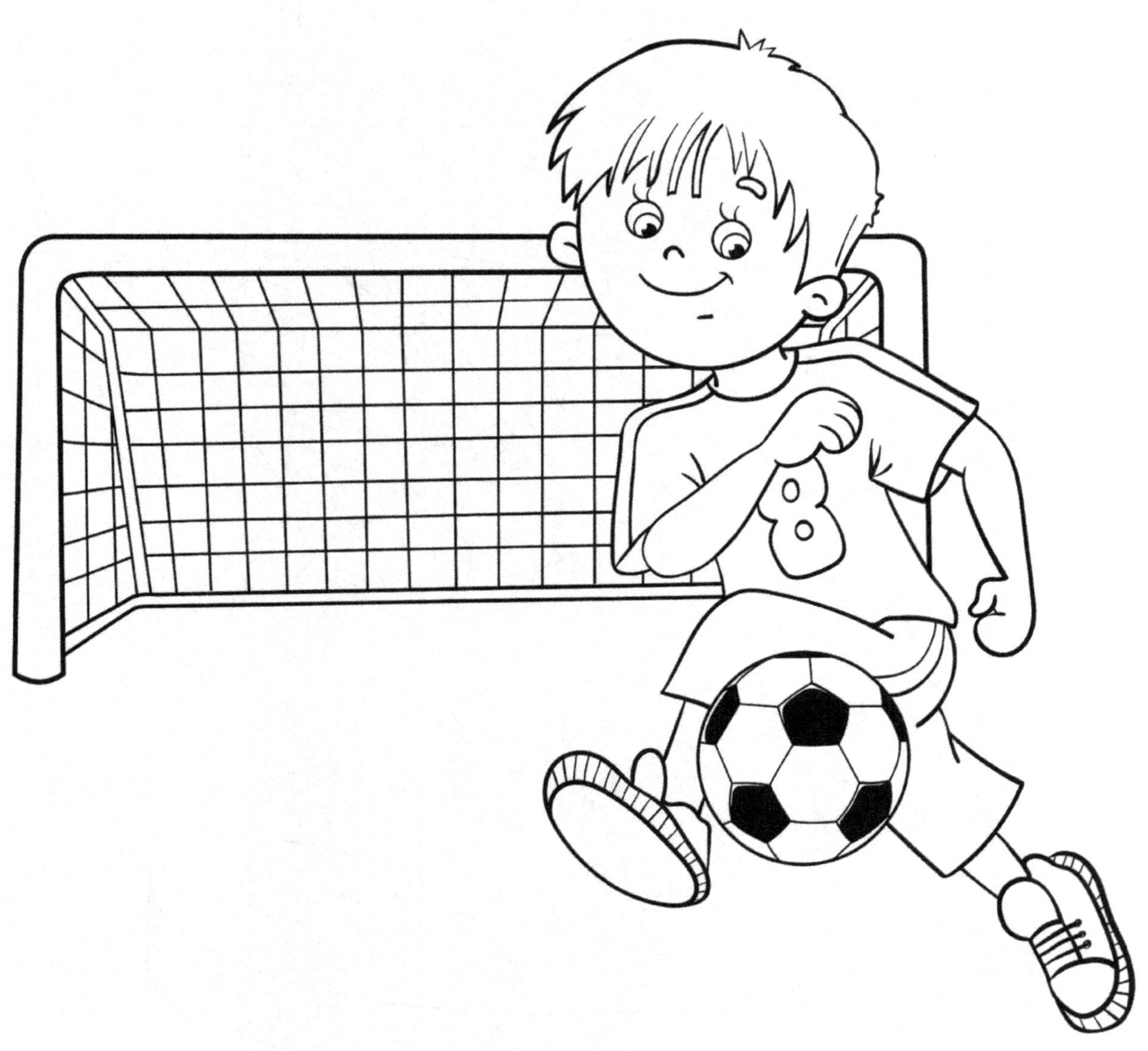

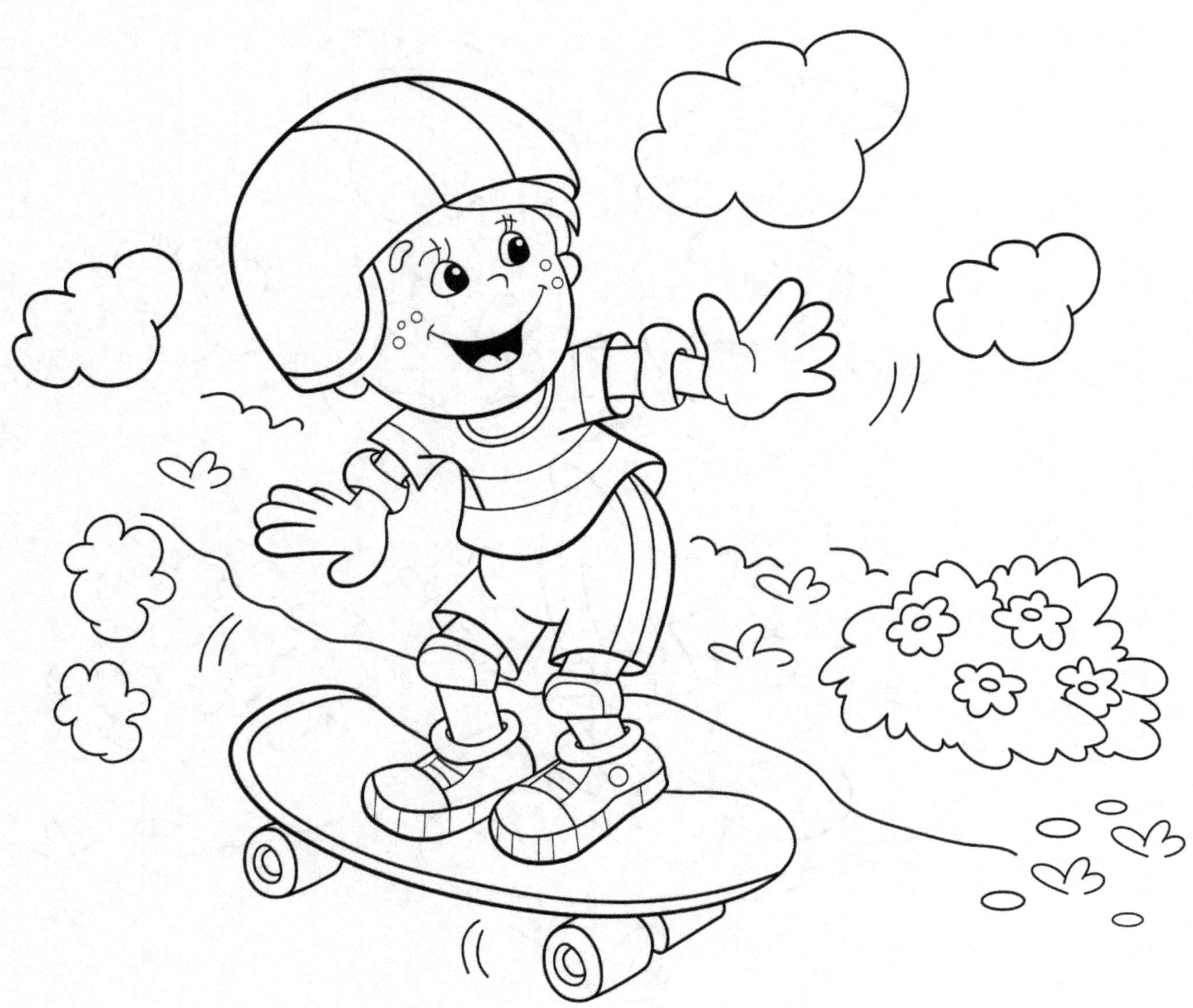

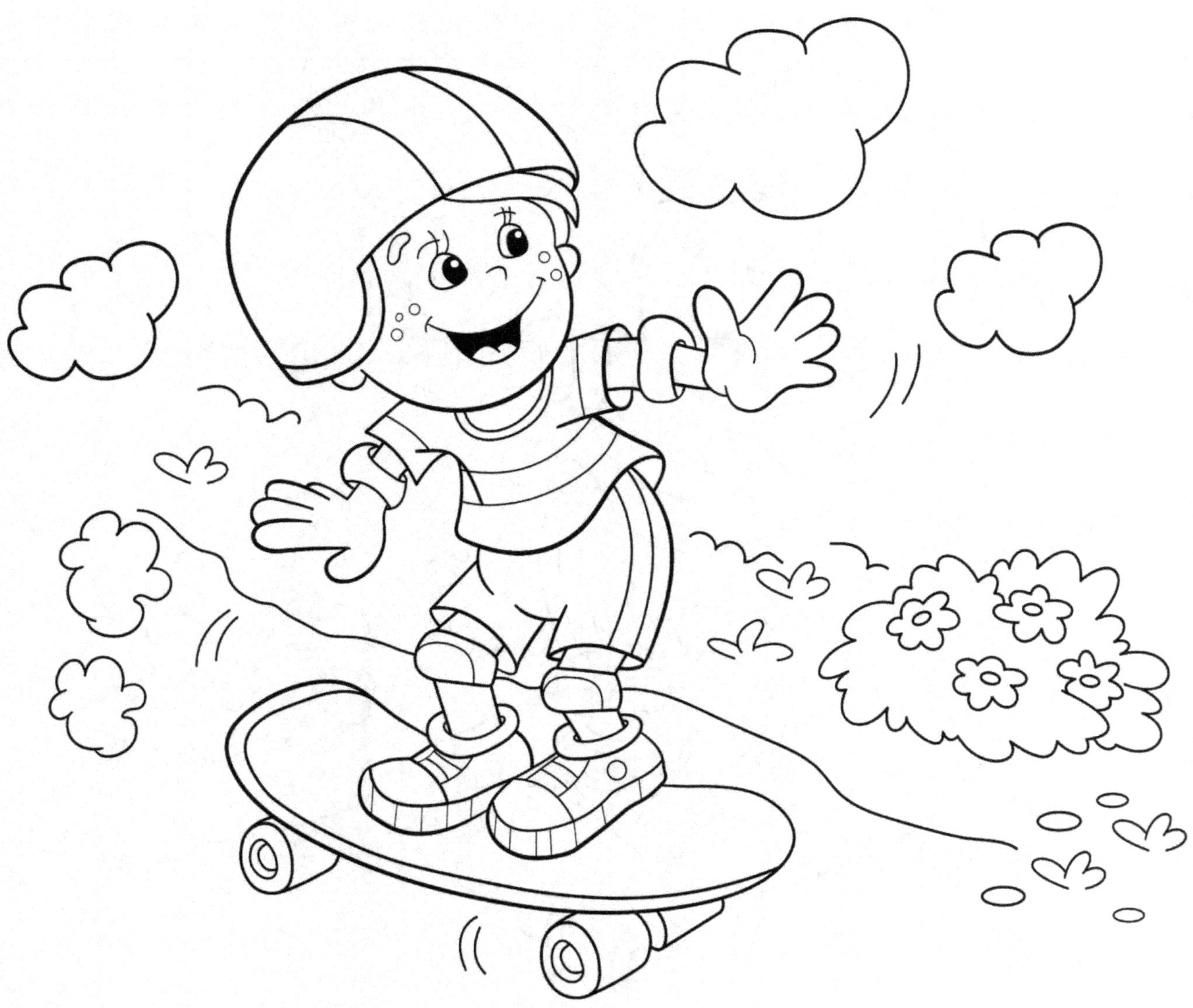

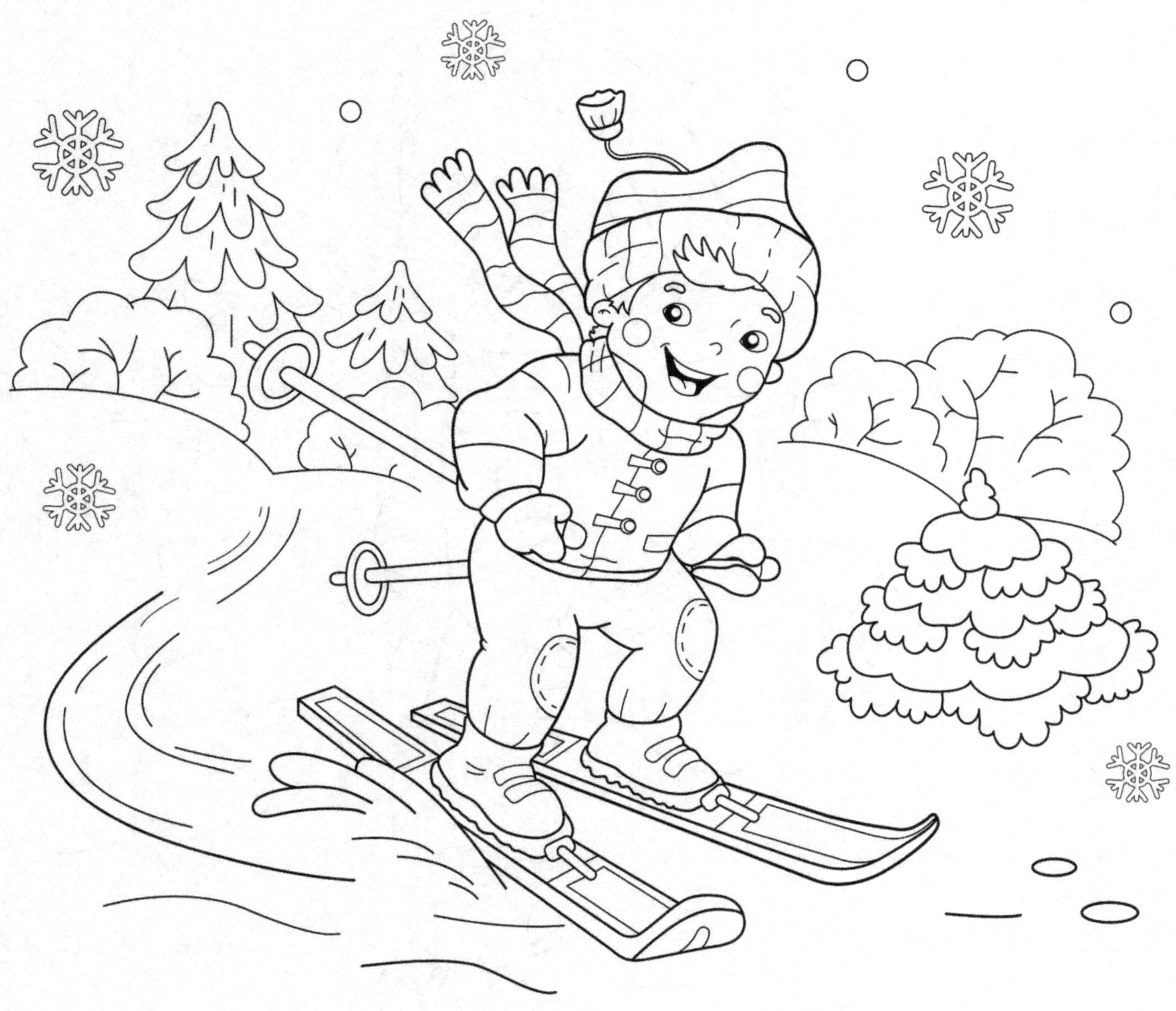

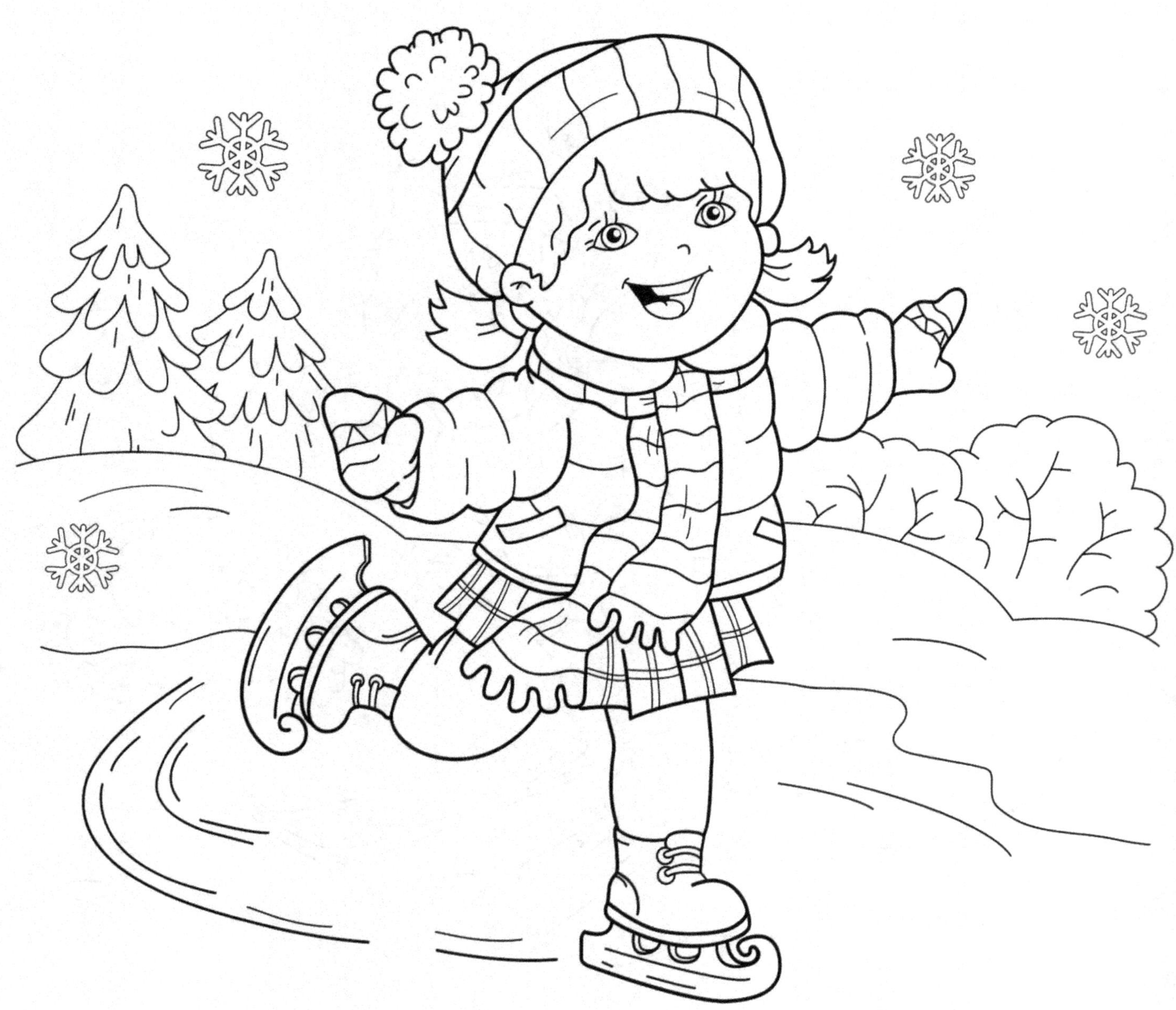

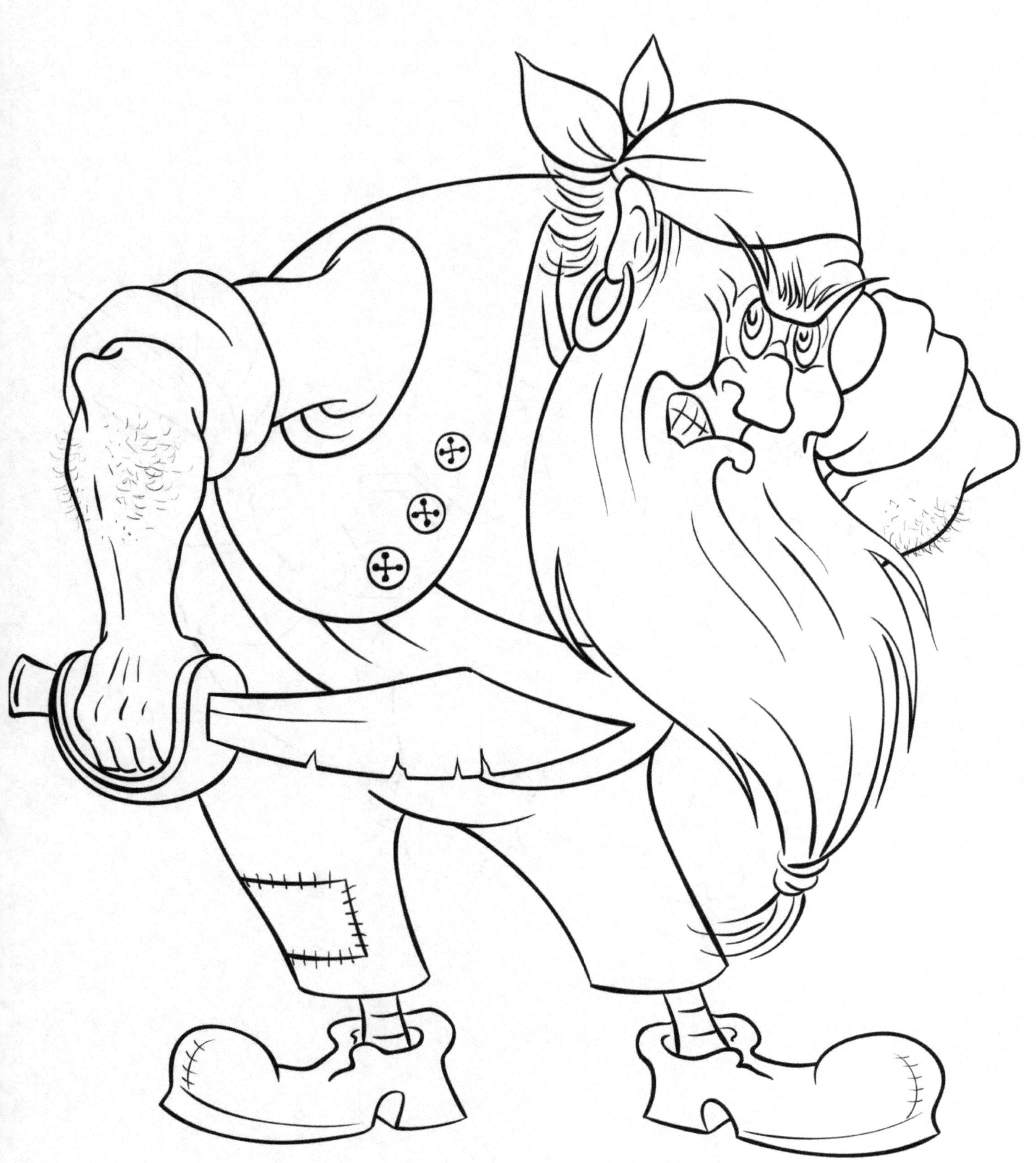

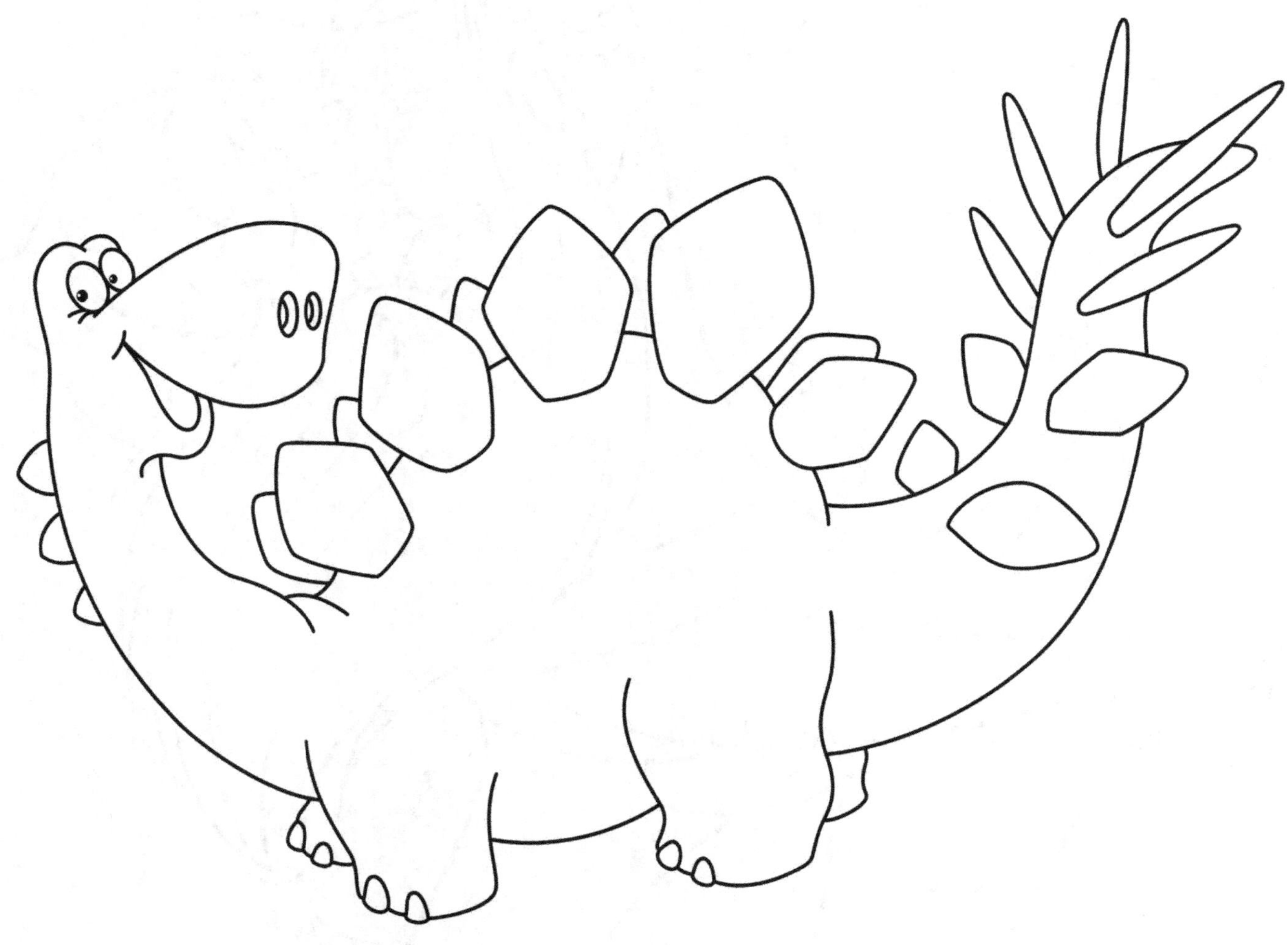

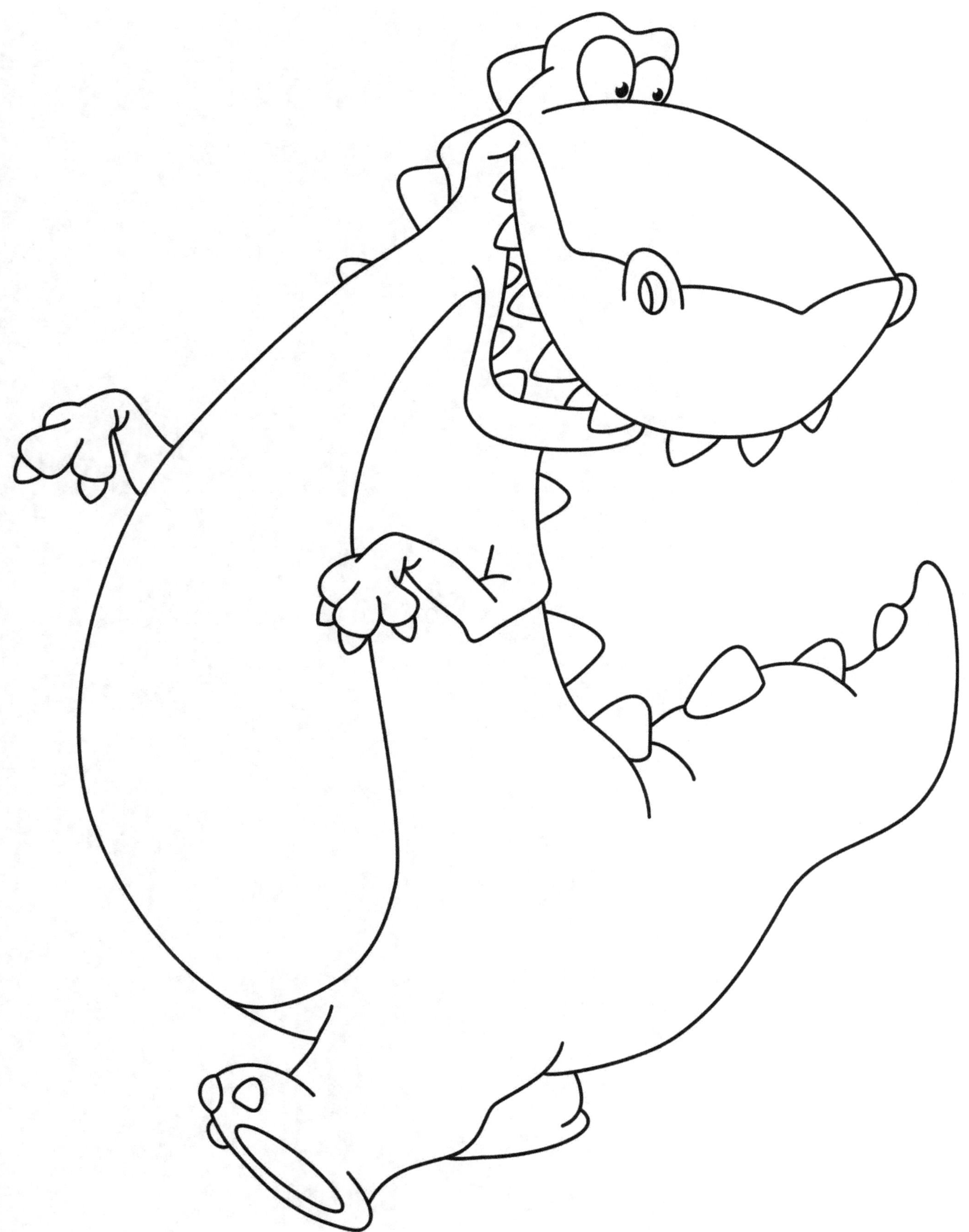